The Enigma of Shadow Weave
Illuminated

The Enigma of Shadow Weave Illuminated

Understanding Classic Drafts for Inspired Weaving Today

Rebecca Winter

4880 Lower Valley Road • Atglen, PA 19310

Other Schiffer Books on Related Subjects:

Frances L. Goodrich's Brown Book of Weaving Drafts, Barbara Miller with Deb Schillo, ISBN 978-0-7643-4541-8

Archie Brennan: Tapestry as Modern Art, Archie Brennan, as told to Brenda Osborn, ISBN 978-0-7643-6249-1

Ondulé Textiles: Weaving Contours with a Fan Reed, Norma Smayda with Gretchen White, ISBN 978-0-7643-5358-1

Copyright © 2022 by Rebecca Winter

Library of Congress Control Number: 2021948646

Photographs by Clinton Whiting or by the author unless otherwise credited.

Woven works shown appear by permission of the artists.

Permission for use of images and drafts from the *Shuttle Craft Guild Bulletin* by Mary Meigs Atwater granted by Betty Biehl McAlear, granddaughter.

Drafts for Coral Challenge Scarf, Kitchen Towel, and Fingertip Towel are from *1000 (+) Patterns in 4, 6, and 8 Harness Shadow Weaves* by Marian Powell.

All rights reserved. No part of this work may be reproduced or used in any form or by any means—graphic, electronic, or mechanical, including photocopying or information storage and retrieval systems—without written permission from the publisher.

The scanning, uploading, and distribution of this book or any part thereof via the Internet or any other means without the permission of the publisher is illegal and punishable by law. Please purchase only authorized editions and do not participate in or encourage the electronic piracy of copyrighted materials.

"Schiffer," "Schiffer Publishing, Ltd.," and the pen and inkwell logo are registered trademarks of Schiffer Publishing, Ltd.

Cover and interior design by Ashley Millhouse
Type set in Fira Sans/Mrs Eaves XL Serif
Front jacket photo by Clinton Whiting. Rust and blue green scarf, courtesy of Julie Gerrard. Two blue and multicolored scarves, courtesy of Cynthia Newman. Two rust and tan scarves, courtesy of Vila Cox.
Cover photo by the author. Detail, Tapestry #1—Nine Patch Two (Rebecca Winter).

ISBN: 978-0-7643-6204-0
Printed in India

Published by Schiffer Publishing, Ltd.
4880 Lower Valley Road
Atglen, PA 19310
Phone: (610) 593-1777; Fax: (610) 593-2002
Email: Info@schifferbooks.com
Web: www.schifferbooks.com

For our complete selection of fine books on this and related subjects, please visit our website at www.schifferbooks.com. You may also write for a free catalog.

Schiffer Publishing's titles are available at special discounts for bulk purchases for sales promotions or premiums. Special editions, including personalized covers, corporate imprints, and excerpts, can be created in large quantities for special needs. For more information, contact the publisher.

We are always looking for people to write books on new and related subjects. If you have an idea for a book, please contact us at proposals@schifferbooks.com.

Courtesy of Vila Cox

This book is dedicated to the Handweavers Guild of Boise Valley—the group and its inimitable members.

Contents

Preface: The Enigma of Shadow Weave 12

Acknowledgments 15

Chapter 1. Introduction to Shadow Weave 17

The Beginnings of Shadow Weave and Historical References	18
Atwater Drafting-Method Reference Summary	23
Powell Drafting-Method Reference Summary	24

Chapter 2. What Is Shadow Weave? 27

The Two Main Defining Shadow Weave Characteristics	28
Shadow Weave Characteristics List	32

Chapter 3. Basic Design Considerations 35

Defining Color-and-Weave	35
Value—a Color Theory Element	36
Hue, Color, and Contrast of Hue	37
Optical Mixing	38
Simultaneous Contrast	38
Scale	38
Distance	39
Draft Conventions	39
Valid Cloth Definition	41
Sett for Shadow Weave	41
Distinction between Rising and Sinking Shed Tie-Ups	41
Management of Selvages	43
No Possible Plain Weave in Atwater or Powell Shadow Weave	46
Parallel Shadow Weave	48
Extended Twill	48

Chapter 4. Designing Shadow Weave with the Atwater Method 51

How to Draft Shadow Weave with the Atwater Method   51
Atwater's First Drafts from the *Shuttle-Craft Guild Bulletin*   55

Chapter 5. Powell Conversion and Drafting 73

Chapter 6. Block Theory and Shadow Weave 81

Profile Drafts   82
Atwater Shadow Weave Units   84
Powell Shadow Weave Units   85
A Unidirectional Draft   86
Symmetrical Drafts and Point Twill Fashion Adjustments   86
Shared Units   87
Asymmetrical Drafts   89
The Design Blocks Weave Together   91
The Order of the Colors within the Units   95
The Rules for Shadow Weave within Block Theory   96
The Trouble with Shadow Weave as a Block Weave—Ahh! The Enigma   97

Chapter 7. Designing Shadow Weave 99

Extending Shadow Weave   100
Switch Draft   102
Designing with Profile Drafts   105
Options for Changing and Working with Units   107
Multiple-Shaft Shadow Weave   113
Does Shadow Weave Make Lace?   114
Using Other Types of Design Contrast   116

Chapter 8. Doubleweave?...........................125

    Is There Doubleweave in Shadow Weave?   126
    From What Structure Did Atwater Derive Shadow Weave?   128

Chapter 9. Shadow Weave Projects.................131

    Words of Wisdom   132
    My Profile Drafts   133
    Projects: Three Scarves and Three Towels   134

Coral Challenge Scarf   136

Gray & Brown Scarf   140

8/2 Tencel Scarf   144

Kitchen Towel   148

Fingertip Towel   152

Tea Towel   156

Once More about Finishing Shadow Weave   159

Chapter 10. A Shadow Weave Synopsis 161

    The Lists   162
    Atwater or Powell?   162
    The Structure of Shadow Weave   162

Conclusion 164

Bibliography 166

Appendixes 168

    Appendix A. Shadow Weave Sett Chart   168
    Appendix B. Additional Atwater Drafts   170
    Appendix C. Three Methods of Creating the Same Exact Cloth   188

Index 191

Preface

The Enigma of Shadow Weave

There is a resurgence of interest in shadow weave today, and prior to this book the emphasis has been for the most part on the parallel threadings and treadlings of Mary Meigs Atwater (1878–1956). The last time large amounts of this book's content was published, it was by Marian Powell in 1976. My preferred method of weaving shadow weave is the method Marian Powell proposed. Her threadings and treadlings are sequential. You will learn about the theory of the weave here, and then you will be able to design your own shadow weave drafts from profiles using the Powell method.

I like to wax lyrical when I think about my creative work. There is a whole scenario in my head about how shadow weave is an enigma, which led to the title of this book. How can the light exist at the same time as the dark? How can there be so many ways to weave shadow weave? Is it twill, or is it plain weave? How was it invented? Was it even invented at all? My wish is that you become as fascinated with finding these answers as I remain.

At the beginning of my journey with shadow weave I didn't know what I didn't know. And there have been various "aha" moments that moved me closer to the illumination. When weaving my first Powell shadow weave cloth, I could understand the first twill line. However, the reason for the next out-of-order line in the threading and treadling escaped me. I pondered and worked on that mystery for some weeks. Then one day I was reading more about shadow weave, and the answer just popped clearly into my mind. This was a significant "aha" moment. And I have to say in reality it was a "duh" moment, because once I could see it, the answer was so very simple. This was the first of many moments when the light shone.

An example of shadow weave's impact on the viewer occurred with a friend who is a nonweaver. There was a potluck social gathering with several friends. I knew these people were interested in what I was weaving at the time, so I took a piece of shadow weave to show them. When explaining to my nonweaver friend about the featherstitching—that it is dark on one side and light on the other—she said, "Oh, wow." Then I pointed out the hatching is horizontal on one side and vertical on the other, and she said, "What!!!" She was clearly astounded. She looked again, as if it were some kind of magic. Mysterious or not, this is the power that shadow weave's enigma holds!

Even the inventor of shadow weave, Mary Meigs Atwater, promoted the mystery of shadow weave. She wrote in her *Shuttle-Craft Guild Bulletin* she planned to keep it as something she would share only with her guild members. She even challenged those outside the fold to derive a draft for it—a difficult task, by her estimation. Both she and Harriet Tidball, who was responsible for the reintroduction of shadow weave in her tenure of writing for the *Shuttle-Craft Guild Bulletin*, wrote about the difficulty of deriving a draft from merely visualizing the cloth.

The name of the weave itself alludes to an air of mystery. What lies there in the shadows? May we shed some light to illuminate those shadows? This book is evidence of my pursuit of the light. I hope it brings to light some answers about the nature of shadow weave and how it works for you. Okay, okay, I'll get my brain out of the way so you may begin your own journey.

Welcome to your shadow weave exploration. It is a fascinating weave, whichever method you choose. I invite you to seek the answers to the enigma for yourself.

—Rebecca Winter, Master Weaver

From left: Silk Scarf by the Author. 10/2 Cotton Scarf in Light Rust and 10 Blue Green Courtesy of Julie Gerrard. Two 20/2 Cotton Scarves in Teal and Other Colors, Courtesy of Cynthia Newman. 8/2 Tencel Scarf in Straw and Pompeii, Courtesy of Vila Cox.

Acknowledgments

I would like to thank the following. Without them, bringing this book to fruition would have been a much more difficult task:

My weaving artist friends, who agreed to weave shadow weave—Mary Berent, Vila Cox, Cynthia Newman, Julie Gerrard, Greta Ankeny, Marlene Bean, and Jenni Jimmerson.

Clinton Dene Whiting of Clinton Dene Photography for his beautiful photographs.

The Handweavers Guild of America and the Certificate of Excellence Program, for the structure for study.

Connie Griffin, copy editor extraordinaire.

Debra Temple for your unwavering support.

Sandra Korinchak, my editor at Schiffer Publishing.

The groundbreaking weaving designers of history—Marian Powell, Mary Meigs Atwater, and Harriet Tidball, always first and foremost.

CHAPTER 1

Introduction to Shadow Weave

◇◇

Where does one begin to describe shadow weave? It is a color-and-weave cloth. It is based on twill. It can be a unit weave. Both geometric and organic motifs can be woven on one warp. When you change the sett to create a warp-faced cloth, warp-faced rep weave can be woven. There are at least three different drafting methods, which create the exact same cloth.

The Beginning of Shadow Weave and Historical References

Mary Meigs Atwater was responsible for the resurgence of home handweaving during the early to mid-twentieth century. Atwater began teaching wounded veterans of World War I, while she was a member of the army herself. She taught them to weave as a way to help them find a useful occupation. Later she published a correspondence course in handloom weaving, and her students mailed their handwovens to her for evaluation. She offered critique about how the handwovens could be improved. She also published a newsletter for her students, called the *Shuttle-Craft Guild Bulletin*. When one is reading the newsletters, her strict adherence to high standards comes through in no uncertain terms. She frequently states what is good weaving practice, and also just as often, what is not good weaving practice.

Atwater introduced "the 'shadow' weave" in February 1942, in her newsletter. She said she was inspired to develop it because she wanted to find a good weave for the new cotton yarns being manufactured at the time. The home weavers of her guild were much more accustomed to using linen yarn. However, due to the circumstances of World War II, linen yarn had become very difficult to obtain.

In later publications, Atwater said she wanted to keep the method of weaving shadow weave a secret among the Shuttle-Craft Guild members. She stated in her newsletter that those outside the fold of her guild would find it difficult to determine how the shadow weave fabric was woven. This fact created an air of mystery around shadow weave.

A question remains after reading the February 1942 article, which may not be answerable. From what weave structure did Atwater derive shadow weave? This may be the ultimate enigma. At later dates, Harriet Tidball, Mary Black, Clotilde Barrett, Doramay Keasbey, Madelyn van der Hoogt, and Linda Hartshorn published more information about shadow weave. None of these, however, say definitively from what structure shadow weave was derived. Tidball said Atwater most likely derived shadow weave from rep weave. Publications coming after Tidball's also stated Atwater derived shadow weave from rep weave. There is an alternate theory. It is possible Atwater derived shadow weave from doubleweave.

In her first article, Mary Meigs Atwater describes the weave by saying, "I am calling the weave given in drafts (a), (b), and (c) the 'shadow' weave, for obvious reasons. It is essentially plain tabby weave without any skips except the little two thread skips that make the light and dark outlines between the changes of hatching." This was the first mention and naming of the shadow weave. The statement about "obvious reasons" relates to the designs where we have light on one side of the motif and dark on the other, which creates the effect of a shadow. While Atwater gives a description of the cloth created, she does not describe how her drafts were developed or derived.

Marian Powell was another innovator in the development of shadow weave. There is no biography that I have found about Powell. The only information about her life is gleaned from her publications about shadow weave. The early publications cited her location as Perry, Iowa. Later publications, some of which may be found through the Handweavers Guild of America, cite her as living in Ajijic, Jalisco, Mexico. Actually, the timing of these publications is assumed on my part, as well, because there are no dates listed. The assumptions were formed from following how the weave morphed and changed from the early publications in the *Shuttle-Craft Guild Bulletin* to how they were presented later in her book, which will be discussed further in the two "Reference Summary" sections in this chapter. Powell's significant innovation offered a completely different drafting system that creates the exact same cloth as Atwater's drafting system.

The Atwater method of drafting shadow weave is best for ease of designing from twills. The Powell method may serve best for ease of threading and treadling. Both of these theories of drafting shadow weave will be discussed and examined.

Historical References

There is very little evidence of anything like Atwater's shadow weave in prior publications. Atwater actually says in her first article, on page 2, "and though one hesitates to claim that anything is 'new' in weaving I have never seen anything like these weaves in my rather extensive browsings and with me at least they are original."

In one reference, *Die farbige Gewebemusterung*, by Franz Donat, there is the draft seen below on the left. This volume is a book in German about color-and-weave, published in 1907. With just a couple of adjustments to the Donat draft, we can create the Powell shadow weave draft shown on the right.

The first adjustment to the Donat draft was made in the tie-up—it was inverted and then rotated. The second adjustment was made to the treadling color way. It was changed to begin with light, which is the same as the threading. These two drafts produce the same cloth, if reversed and rotated.

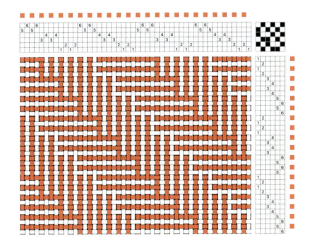

Donat draft #XXXVI, 2. Also found as draft #63823 at handweaving.net.

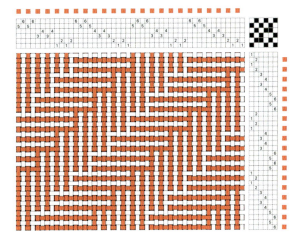

Draft with Powell tie-up

There are several other color-and-weave drafts in the book by Donat that have the one dark and one light colorway. However, they require multiple shafts with fancy twill tie-ups. One example of these is shown below.

Another interesting photo is found in the book *Textile Design and Colour*, by William Watson, which was first published in 1912. Older books such as these include drafts that are somewhat inaccessible to the handweaver because they require a great many shafts to produce the designs.

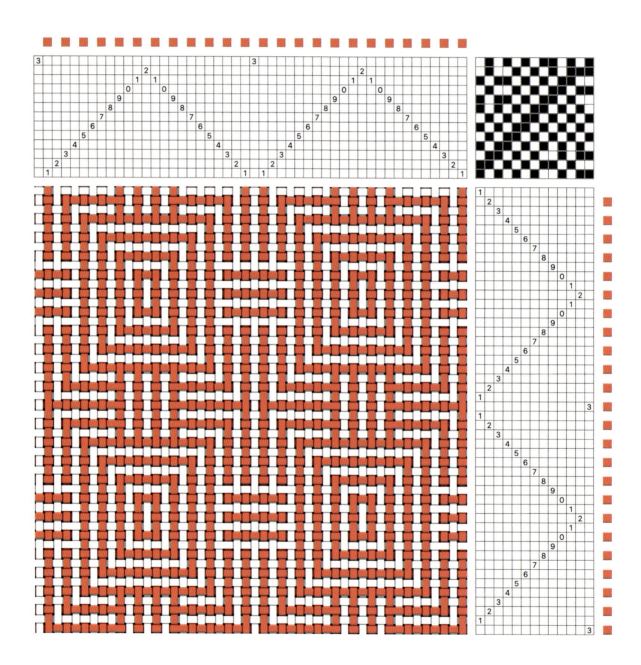

Donat draft #XXXVI, 6; draft #63827 at handweaving.net

Figure 234 in the Watson book, below left, is no exception. It does offer something to ponder in relation to shadow weave, however. Clearly, if we were to create the draft for it, a great many shafts would be required, due to the many and varied curves. The cloth shown in the photo was most likely woven on a Jacquard loom, which creates very intricate designs. Figure 235, *below right*, is the draft for only a portion of the photo. It alone requires thirty-nine shafts and thirty-seven treadles. If you visualize rotating it right once and place it in the upper left portion of figure 234, you find an approximation of the patterning (1912).

Watson's book can be found on the website handweaving.net in its entirety. The draft for the Watson fabric was also found (2018) on this website, which offers drafts in the form of .wif files from older publications. A single repeat is shown on the next page. It is clearly not an Atwater draft and, like those from Donat, has a fancy twill tie-up.

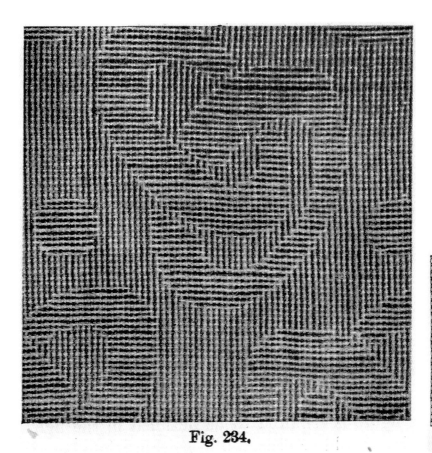

Fig. 234.

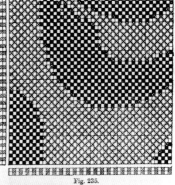

Fig. 235.

Figures from *Textile Design and Colour* by William Watson

The Enigma of Shadow Weave Illuminated

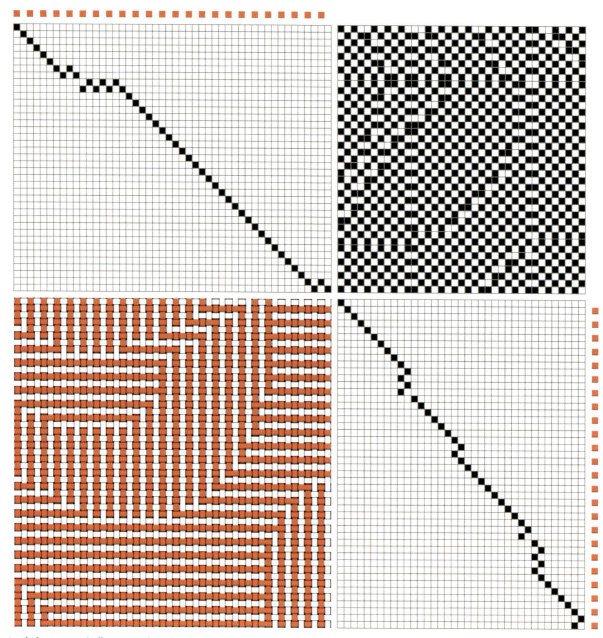

Draft for Watson's figure 235 found at handweaving.net, #62154, one repeat

Another area to research for historical evidence of shadow weave is in Scandinavian publications. Several of these were reviewed in my research, but very little evidence of shadow weave was found. What was found there more closely resembled rep weave and the squarish designs created from such drafts.

Atwater Drafting-Method Reference Summary

Multiple references describe the Atwater method of drafting shadow weave. As a bit of clarification, the *Shuttle-Craft Guild Bulletin* had several name changes over the years. For the discussion here it is considered the same publication.

In 1946, when Atwater needed assistance with the increasing requirements of her growing guild, Harriet Tidball transitioned into the role of editor for Atwater's newsletter. In Tidball's writings there is evidence she maintained the strict high weaving standards begun by Atwater in her community of weavers. Later Tidball was the first, after Atwater, to reintroduce shadow weave in detail in the *Shuttle Craft Guild Handweaver's Bulletin* in June and July 1953. Her articles are concise, clear, and detailed. All the information needed to create shadow weave using the Atwater method are offered in these articles. With this publication, shadow weave was more widely distributed than it was in 1942. As a result, perhaps some of the mystery instilled by Atwater was dispelled by Tidball.

Later, Mary Black assumed the position of coeditor for the bulletin from Tidball, with Joyce Chown as a second coeditor. Black and Chown called the publication *Shuttle Craft*. In the fall of 1959, Black published information about her shadow weave "Experiments." The information in these articles is very basic. They offer a place to start in the study of shadow weave. The information in Black's first article references Atwater's article from February 1942. In the second article, Black expresses chagrin that she did not have access to Tidball's articles from 1953. She offers clarifications and then republished much of Tidball's information exactly as it was written in 1953.

Clotilde Barrett published information about shadow weave in her periodical called *Weaver's Journal* in late 1976 and early 1977. Then in 1980 she published the monograph called *Shadow Weave and Corkscrew Weave*, with much the same information found in her periodical. In the monograph she describes the process of creating the Atwater parallel draft. She calls the drafts "interlocking," which is another term for parallel drafts. Her approach is mathematical and includes specific formulas for creating parallel drafts.

Lucille Landis, in *Twills and Twill Derivatives* (1977), offers another clear and concise description of shadow weave. The method she describes is the same Atwater method. She also says shadow weave is considered an extension of log cabin.

Madelyn van der Hoogt, in *The Complete Book of Drafting for Handweavers* (1993, page 21), says, "shadow weave looks like twill, but the interlacement is really plain weave with scattered 2-thread floats." She also offers the same description of developing drafts as for the Atwater method.

Doramay Keasbey, in her book called *Pattern Techniques for Handweavers* (2005), offers the same description of drafting with the Atwater parallel method. She also describes some of the same characteristics of shadow weave. She goes on to describe three methods of drafting shadow weave, which are the Atwater method, parallel shadow weave, and the Powell method. Drafts from these three methods can be created that weave the exact same cloth.

An article by Linda Hartshorn was published in the May/June 2016 issue of *Heddlecraft*. Both the Atwater and the Powell methods are described.

Powell Drafting-Method Reference Summary

Marian Powell published three articles in the March, April, and May 1960 issues of *Shuttle Craft*. The articles were called "Shadow Weave Conversion." In these articles she offered a way to convert the Atwater drafts into something a little easier to weave. The first article gives details of the conversion. In the subsequent two articles she worked to convert some of the popular twill derivatives, such as honeysuckle, overshot, or crackle, to something like shadow weave.

These early Powell experiments are very rudimentary. It seems Powell was working with the premise that most twill and twill-derivative drafts could be converted to shadow weave. She first made them into Atwater drafts, then applied her new conversion method to them. In her later work, something more distinct, precise, and separate emerged. It is interesting, however, to take a look at where Powell began her exploration, and to compare it to what she created after many years of exploration.

Powell also wrote an article for the *Handweavers & Craftsman* periodical in 1961. Powell's precise manner of study can be seen in this writing. The article outlines thirty drafts to try on one four-shaft threading—a daunting array of samples to weave. These drafts are also quite simple and again rudimentary, much like in her *Shuttle Craft* articles. The significant detail offered by Powell in this article is that she describes her method of drafting as sequential. This represents a key departure from Atwater's method.

There is one type of publication by Powell to discuss that is more obscure. They are called *Four Harness Shadow Weave—Converted Form* and *Multi Harness Shadow Weave—Converted Form*. She mentions on the first page that anyone interested in more information about the conversion method could refer to the *Shuttle Craft* articles of 1960. Her name and address in Perry, Iowa, are printed at the bottom of the first page, along with the cost of each pamphlet with samples—a modest one dollar. Also at the bottom of the page for the multiple-harness versions is typed the title *Multi Harness and Four Harness Shadow Weave Pamphlets*. The pamphlets give one threading and from six to eighteen treadlings for the threadings. There were sixteen four-shaft threadings, three six-shaft threadings, and eight eight-shaft threadings. Unfortunately, there are no dates on these publications.

The first pamphlet discovered consists of three printed pages and fourteen actual black-and-white cloth samples. The draft instruction page is very similar to those found in Powell's book, and includes a threading "short draft" (known today as a profile draft), a full threading, and fifteen different treadlings for this threading. No instructions related to yarn or sett are given. The yarn that was used approximates 10/2 cotton, and because they are precious historical samples, they were not tested to determine exactly what type of yarn was used. One guess about dating, by following the trail of how the drafts are presented, is this publication was offered after the *Shuttle Craft* articles and prior to the book she published in 1976. These samples are much closer to those found in her book than those found in the 1960 articles, although the management of the twill fashion points is not the same.

Additional pamphlet publications were found later. A best guess about the dating of these publications is they were a subsequent group of samples woven to go with the pamphlet instruction pages. The cloth samples in these are not black and white. Instead they are woven with various colors or with novelty yarns, such as metallics or synthetics. Additional treadlings are also offered in this grouping of samples, and additional samples were also woven for these treadlings. As one works more with designing shadow weave, more treadlings occur and are tried. This would certainly have been the case with Powell and her approach to shadow weave. Then she wished to offer these samples as additional ways to work with shadow weave.

Finally, the most important publication by Powell is her book published by Robin and Russ in 1976. This book represents extensive research in the years leading up to the publication. There are 1,236 drafts included in the book, and it is called *1000 (+) Patterns in 4, 6, and 8 Harness Shadow Weaves*. The black-and-white sample photographs show high contrast in the yarns used, although she does not offer yarn or sett information for them. She offers "preferred" and "secondary" drafts. The visual effects created in the drawdowns of the preferred drafts are clearly outlined and symmetrical motifs. The motifs created in the secondary drafts are not as distinctively clear. There are also drafts that Powell calls "switch drafts." Powell continues the use of profile threadings in her book for all the drafts offered. Working from the perspective of using profile drafts within block theory is another departure from Atwater's approach.

One more astonishing attribute of Powell's book is that where she includes actual full shadow weave drafts, the drawdown designs are created on the page by typing or typesetting rows of lowercase "m"s to represent the dark threads with spaces for the light threads. This is an incredibly meticulous method of showing the color-and-weave designs of shadow weave hatching and feather-stitching on a printed page. Can you imagine the focus on detail required to create such a representation of a weaving plan, not to mention the editing to be sure each "m" is in its proper place? There are fifty such drafts in her book.

Personal Preferences

While I am including information about Mary Atwater's shadow weave, because it is essential for creating a complete picture of shadow weave, I have always woven shadow weave by using Marian Powell's methods of drafting. Approaching shadow weave from a standpoint of block theory makes sense to me. Therefore, the draft examples and illustrations in this book are mainly Powell method drafts.

I am a color person who has spent a lot of time learning about weaving structure. This approach of broadening one's view to include all aspects of weaving certainly provides a greater understanding of the whole picture. I would encourage all weavers to adopt it.

You may be more drawn to the Atwater method. Both methods of creating shadow weave are valid. The conversion between Powell and Atwater is included, and moving from one method to the other is easily accomplished.

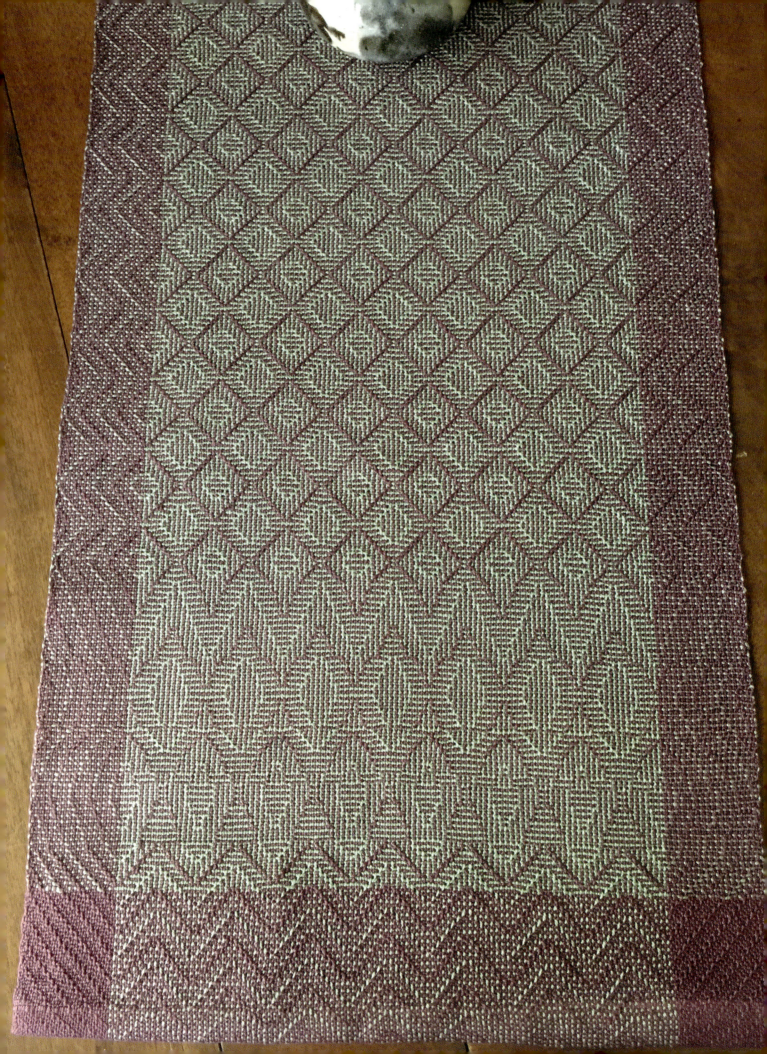

CHAPTER 2

What Is Shadow Weave?

There are certain characteristics and rules that help us understand the intricacies of any weave structure and help us to become adept at producing cloth. That is always the foundation. We learn the rules, and then we know where we can stretch them to our individual designing desire. Let's define where we start with shadow weave.

The Two Main Defining Shadow Weave Characteristics

There are two main characteristics of shadow weave. When taken in combination, the two define the pure form of the weave. First, a large portion of the cloth is plain weave, and hatching or pinstripes are seen in these plain weave areas. In order to create the hatching, the colorway needs to be primarily one dark and one light in both threading and treadling. The hatching occurs both vertically and horizontally, and on the reverse of the cloth the hatching effect occurs in the opposite direction—where it is vertical on one side, it is horizontal on the other, and vice versa.

The second main characteristic is the featherstitching that separates and outlines the areas of plain weave hatching. Harriet Tidball coined the term "featherstitching" in the *Shuttle Craft Guild Handweaver's Bulletin* of July 1953. She said, "The edges of blocks of patterns which are developed like twills consist of interlaced 2-thread floats which raise above the flat base fabric and somewhat resemble featherstitching." In this statement Tidball also emphasized the textural quality of the featherstitching. When the cloth is viewed from the side, particularly with larger yarns, the raised texture of the featherstitching is apparent.

When examining the featherstitching closely, we can isolate one set of the two-thread floats. We see one float in the weft and one in the warp. These two floats occur at right angles to one another.

We can isolate this same configuration in 2/2 twill, as seen in this draft. There are two sets of warp and weft floats indicated within the oval. In this draft, multiple series of these pairs occur diagonally. These diagonal parallel rows are what we recognize as the most distinctive characteristic of straight twill.

In shadow weave we see diagonal rows of these right-angle, warp-and-weft, two-thread floats, with plain weave separating them. These rows are the featherstitching.

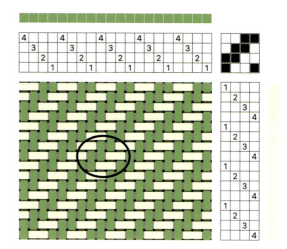

Regular 2/2 straight-twill draft

Hatching

The word "hatching" is an art drawing term that refers to the use of lines drawn parallel to one another to give the effect of shading. This accurately describes the pinstripes of shadow weave, since they appear as parallel lines. Atwater, having been classically trained in art, referred to this color-and-weave effect in shadow weave as "hatching."

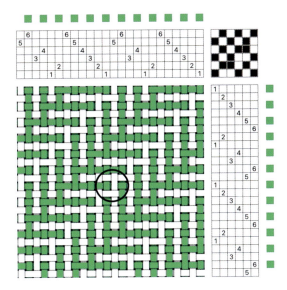

Shadow weave straight-twill fashion draft

One pair of two-thread floats is highlighted in the shadow weave draft, and both of these floats are a light color within the oval. The entire diagonal row of light featherstitching is easily seen extending on either side and through the oval. If we look closely we can also see the diagonal lines of dark featherstitching.

Another attribute of the featherstitching is that where it is dark on one side of the cloth, it is light on the reverse, and vice versa. One layer of the featherstitching interlacement lies above the other. This creates the textural quality of the cloth described by Tidball. There are some interesting conclusions to make from examining this fascinating structural effect, which we'll look at in chapter 8.

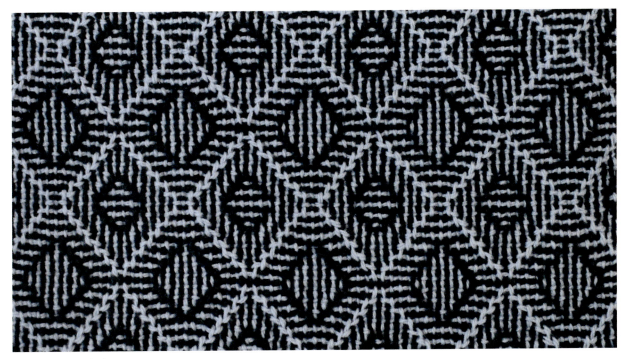

Shadow weave cloth

An example of hand-embroidered featherstitching

Here is an example of hand-embroidered featherstitching. When compared to the featherstitching created in shadow weave, there is a distinct similarity.

The two-thread floats also occur around the edges of square patterning in the cloth. In the draft we easily see the white two-thread floats on the left and top of the central figure—the light threads. The floats are also present on the right and under the central figure in the dark threads.

Whether we call these vertical and horizontal two-thread floats featherstitching may be in question, since they no longer appear similar to the embroidery. Powell (1976) and Barrett (1980) refer only to the diagonal rows by the name of "featherstitching."

Powell refers to this square or rectangular visual patterning as the "block formation" (1976, page 4). This, however, should not be confused with block theory.

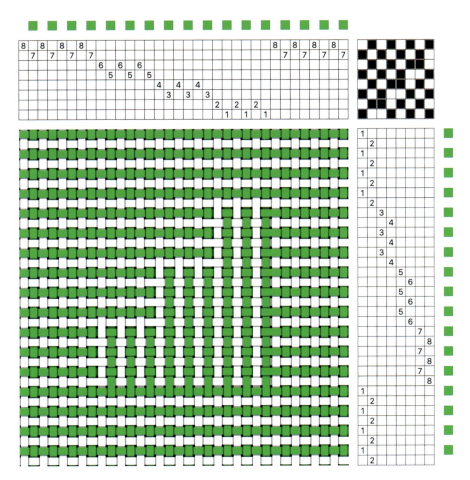

Square patterning shadow weave draft

Tidball's Featherstitching

Tidball called the diagonal lines "featherstitching" only in the 1953 *Shuttle Craft Guild Handweaver's Bulletin* articles. In later publications, such as her books *The Weaver's Book* and *The Handloom Weaves*, she does not use this term. In *The Handloom Weaves*, enlarged edition, on page 41, she offers a typical description of the plain weave hatching, and then she states further that "the pattern blocks are outlined by two-thread floats which add emphasis and texture interest" (1957/1984). One wonders if she regretted the use of the term "featherstitching" as a descriptor for what happens in shadow weave.

Shadow Weave Characteristics List

While the two main characteristics define the weave, there are others to consider. This list, which includes the two main characteristics, will help you understand and begin to walk through the complexities of shadow weave.

1. Shadow weave is a subset of the larger category of color-and-weave and creates a color-and-weave effect.

2. Most of the time, dark and light alternate one thread by one thread in both the warp and the weft. This value contrast is required for the color-and-weave effect to occur.

3. Hatching occurs in the plain weave areas of the cloth. These appear as vertical and horizontal pinstripes.

4. Hatching is reversed on the reverse side of the cloth. Where it is vertical on one side, it is horizontal on the reverse.

5. Shadow weave is a firm and solid fabric, as a result of the plain weave areas present in the cloth.

6. A sett for plain weave is preferred and a balanced weave is obtained. This is one in which generally the ends per inch are the same as the picks per inch.

7. Intersections of two-thread floats occur on the surface of the cloth, which outline the plain weave hatching areas. This characteristic is called featherstitching.

8. Featherstitching is especially evident in drafts that create a diagonal line in the visual patterning.

9. The two-thread floats still occur when the patterning is not diagonal, and form a square or rectangular visual patterning. For this motif the floats create a ribbed structure.

10. The two-thread float or featherstitching color is reversed on the reverse side of the cloth. It is light on one side and dark on the other.

11. An increase in the number of shafts increases the space of plain weave between the featherstitching lines.

12. Shadow weave is a two-shuttle weave.

13. Smooth yarns function best for shadow weave.

14. No true plain weave is possible across the entire cloth in either the Atwater or the Powell methods.

15. Selvages are consistently inconsistent.

16. An even number of shafts are required.

17. A textured cloth is created; that is evident where the featherstitching creates ridges above the plain weave base.

18. Drafts may be derived from twills, or they may also be derived from profiles.

19. Specific tie-ups are used.

    The Atwater method uses a balanced twill tie-up, in which half the shafts are working opposite the other half in consecutive order. Examples of these are 2/2 twill on four shafts or 4/4 twill on eight shafts.

    The Powell method uses tie-ups specific to the method, which are also balanced.

20. Adjustments need to be made when designing from point twills to create symmetry. These may be called the exceptions or the incidentals.

21. Asymmetrical shadow weave may also be created, and this weave requires no adjustments.

22. Some references refer to shadow weave as a block weave; however, the weave does not fit neatly within block theory. Overall, it would be considered a nonunit structure.

23. Unidirectional shadow weave, on the other hand, is a unit weave.

24. When we do consider shadow weave within block theory, certain parameters or rules apply, and adjustments may need to be made.

25. Where the featherstitching occurs, there are two layers of cloth, or doubleweave.

26. The same exact cloth can be obtained from three different drafts or drafting methods.

Shadow Weave and Log Cabin

The hatching in shadow weave is a characteristic shared by the weave called log cabin. However, log cabin is only plain weave and does not create the second main characteristic of shadow weave—the featherstitching.

Tidball says, in the *Shuttle Craft Guild Handweaver's Bulletin* of July 1953, that shadow weave is based on log cabin. Others, including Barrett, Landis, Windeknecht, and Keasbey, offer similar descriptions. The two do have similarities; however, we need to be more specific. Log cabin should not be called by the name of shadow weave. They are actually two separate and distinct entities. In Atwater's outspoken manner, may I offer this opinion? Saying shadow weave is based on log cabin is like saying twill is based on plain weave. One could use that logic, but it is certainly an oversimplification.

CHAPTER 3

Basic Design Considerations

◇◇◇

Defining Color-and-Weave

Shadow weave is a type or subset of color-and-weave. Color-and-weave is also called color effect or color-and-weave effect. It occurs when there is a combining of two elements of weaving. These two elements are the weave structure and the use of two contrasting yarns as stripes in both the warp and the weft. A visual patterning is created that is seemingly unrelated to the weave structure or the use of color. The most common type of contrast employed to create the effect is value, or the contrast of light versus dark. In color-and-weave, the effect is created within the interaction between the viewer's eye and the surface patterning of the cloth. Simply, it is a visual effect. Hyphenating the term "color-and-weave" differentiates it from "color in weaving," which is merely how we use color in our weaving.

Value—a Color Theory Element

Value, as defined in color theory, is the lightness or darkness of a color or hue. Value is considered by most color theorists to be the most important aspect of color design. Humans respond first to value when viewing whatever they encounter. Our response to light and dark is one of our primal survival instincts. If we can differentiate the dark shapes lurking out there in the night from the lighter spaces, we survive.

Value is also relative. One hue must be placed near another for the value difference to be evident. It is in the relationship of one to the other that value is defined. For example, the same medium hue can appear as either a dark or a light value, depending on the value of the neighboring hue. Here's an illustration of this concept.

Another aspect of value in color theory is that light values appear to advance forward to the eye of the viewer. Dark values recede. This is the result of the reflective quality of the hue. White has 100% reflection. Black has 0% reflection. It is the light reflected back to our eye that creates our perception of color. Color-and-weave utilizes this aspect, since the light motif is usually what we see first. The light values "pop out," so to speak.

Again, if we examine the illustration, the smaller blue-green square on the darker background appears to be positioned forward from the surrounding color. The blue-green square on the lighter-blue background seems to be floating behind.

Value contrast is essential in the creation of the color-and-weave effect in shadow weave. Of course, color-and-weave can be created by using other types of contrast, such as contrast of hue. However, value contrast is the best way to create the effect to its fullest.

Methods to determine how the value of yarns compares include making windings on mat board or plying the two yarns together in a small hank. Or take a photo using the black-and-white camera function on your smartphone or tablet. Sometimes this exercise with our electronic devices gives us surprising results. The sensation of hue does influence our perception of value, and when we remove it, we can see the true value.

 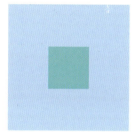

The blue-green square in the center is the exact same hue.

Methods used to determine value contrast

Hue, Color, and Contrast of Hue

A hue is defined as the family name of a color. The term "hue" is more specific than the term "color," although in practice we tend to use them interchangeably. Perception of color is a function of biology and physics. We perceive color only as an interaction between our eye, the surface being viewed, and our brain. Our eyes receive the reflected light from a surface, and our brain interprets the information being received. It is a sensation of light.

On a color wheel, the greater the distance between two colors, the more dissimilar they are. Complementary colors are 180 degrees, or opposite, from each other on the color wheel and therefore have the highest contrast of hue.

Red and green are an example of one of these complementary pairs. They generally are considered to be of about the same value in their pure form. They may offer an effective option for use in shadow weave, because of their contrast of hue.

The exact colors used in the sample below are Lunatic Fringe Yarns, 5 Red and 5 Blue Green. We are seeing the effect of value in this sample since the green is a lighter value. Of course, this accentuates the color-and-weave effect.

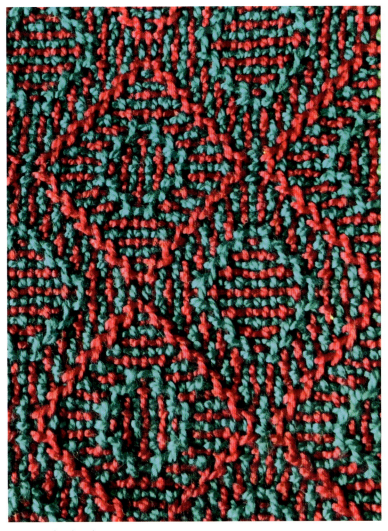

Sample of red and green

Optical Mixing

Optical mixing is another concept to consider when discussing shadow weave as a type of color-and-weave. Pointillism in the world of art is an example. It is a painting technique using dots to create the patterning of an image, and instead of the paint being stirred together on a palette, dots are applied to the surface beside each other. It is the eye that perceives the blending to create color, hue, or shapes in the painting. Yellow dots and blue dots applied together creates a sensation of green.

Another example of this today is the image we see on our electronic devices. If we take the image down to pixels, the same phenomenon is occurring there, since the blending of dots gives us the perception of color.

How does this relate to weaving? As one weft of one color crosses over and under the warps of another color, especially in plain weave, we are creating dots of color on the surface of the cloth. The dots blend and mix to influence how the eye and the brain perceive the fabric. Then, when some of the dots are light and some are dark, the dots join with other areas of their respective value to create a motif, line, or other shape.

Simultaneous Contrast

Simultaneous contrast is related to optical mixing, since it occurs as an interaction between the eye and a patterned surface. It is a complex concept well worth investigating, and involves how our perception of color is affected by placing one color next to another color. This is the concept in play that creates the effects we saw in the example showing the advancing and receding of differing values of color in the discussion about value.

There is a shimmer that occurs that makes us blink or look away. Think of the stark, shimmering black-and-white images created in the op art movement. Black and white are of the highest contrast of value. When designs using black and white are placed next to one another, as in op art, we see and experience examples of simultaneous contrast. The surface seems to shimmer and morph as our eye responds and travels over the surface of the work. There are many examples of op art online.

There are times when the phenomenon of simultaneous contrast occurs during the weaving of a color-and-weave cloth. It is a bit like seeing a rainbow when this occurs—a rare and goose-bump-causing sight. The warp and weft are two distinct colors, but a third color shimmers over the surface of the cloth.

Scale

Scale indicates how large or small something is. It is also related to the concept of proportion. Scale, when taken hand in hand with proportion, is relative, just like value. Some items may be considered small or large depending on something else nearby. It also may depend on some idea or previous experience we have in mind. For example, our idea of a stuffed toy elephant is much different than that of the real living elephant.

In shadow weave it is important to consider the scale of the motifs created. Do you want a dainty, small motif for an article for a baby, or a larger, bold motif for an evening stole? The size of the yarn used affects this concept, of course. Finer yarns obviously create smaller motifs.

Distance

The distance of the viewer from the woven cloth also influences the perception of scale. An all-over pattern from far away can appear homogeneous, with no distinctive motif. However, as one gets closer, the smaller details become more apparent and motifs can be distinguished more easily. Also, it may be best to view fabrics made of finer yarns closer in order to distinguish the intricate patterning achieved with shadow weave. We can also influence the perception of motifs in this cloth by increasing the value contrast of the yarns.

Powell says the following in her book *1000 (+) Patterns in 4, 6, and 8 Harness Shadow Weaves*, on page 4: "Distance at which piece is to be viewed is of utmost importance" (1976). If we experiment with this concept a little, we find value contrast is less apparent the farther away from the cloth we move. Powell says if we are planning to weave curtains to be seen from across the room and would like to evaluate how they may be seen while the cloth is still on the loom, we could use a reducing glass or look at the fabric through the lens of a camera. She also says, "Squinting helps." She does warn us not to climb up on ladders to view the fabric from above, since that would be a bit too dangerous. Again, for evaluating our perception of distance, we can employ our electronic devices to easily zoom in and out to obtain a sense of distance.

Draft Conventions

As we know, there are different ways to read a weaving draft—left to right, top to bottom, and so on. The approach used in this book is to read them from the place on the draft where the threading, the tie-up, the treadling, and the drawdown intersect. In the draft conventions illustration at right, this spot is indicated by the red "X." Start there and read outward into each of the four sections of our draft grid. For example, when treadling, read from the top down.

In reality, when we are working with color-and-weave we need six sections in our drafts. We must include the two colorways for the threading and the treadling. When we consider our definition of color-and-weave, the colorways are very important entities in our drafts and our weaving.

A numeric representation its used in the threading and the treadling. This helps match the numbers to the treadles or shafts when weaving or dressing the loom. The tie-up, on the other hand, is represented primarily without the numbers. This is done so that we can visualize the patterning more easily there, with the high contrast of the black and white squares.

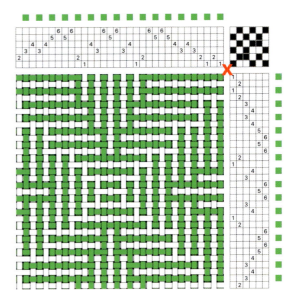

Draft conventions illustration

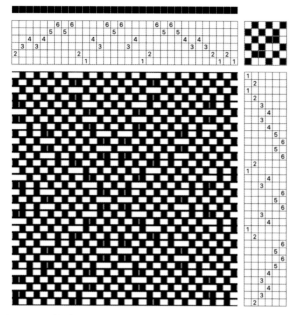

Structure draft

Another valuable draft to use when studying color-and-weave is the structure draft. It shows what the draft would look like without the colorway. We can see a better representation of the underlying interlacement of the cloth, because we are not distracted by the visual patterning created by the colorway. For these drafts, black will be used for the threading and white for the treadling. The white in the treadling does not show in the grid of the graphics from the software; however, we will assume the weft is white in the structure drafts. At left is the structure draft of our color-and-weave draft with the red "X."

Drafts in this book will be limited to eight shafts or fewer, and all the drafts are intended for rising shed looms. The capability and possibility for variety of exploration on this number of shafts are nearly limitless in shadow weave.

Shaft vs. Harness

And yet another convention employed is the use of the word "shaft," which refers to the frames in the center of the loom that hold the heddles. "Shaft" is the more acceptable term used in sources of drafts today and is the term used here.

When I was first learning to weave, the common name was "harness," which remains the term more commonly and currently used within my own community of weavers. We use this term interchangeably with "shaft." I make note of this because many of the historical authors reviewed for the study leading up to this book use the term "harness," including Atwater, Tidball, and Barrett. Then, interestingly, Powell uses the word "shaft."

I understand that "shaft" is considered the more accurate term to describe this part of the loom. I also love the richness of our weaving language, and so I would prefer to follow history, if given the choice.

Valid Cloth Definition

As a weaving teacher, I give advice about the validity of the cloth to my students. As weavers, we should make cloth that meets a certain standard. What is that standard? When evaluating any handwoven cloth, including shadow weave, it is important to determine whether it will stand up to the use for which it is intended. Is it sturdy and well sett? Does it have a nice hand (which is the feel or handling quality of the cloth)? Does it drape nicely as for a scarf, or is it more sturdy as for a rug? If the cloth meets these criteria, we call it valid cloth.

We sometimes call the opposite of valid cloth "sleazy." One test to determine sleazy cloth is to gently push your finger into the cloth. If it opens over your finger, it may be called "sleazy." On the other hand, there are some beautiful handwoven fabrics done in the Saori style, which are wonderfully open and gauzy. These fabrics are commonly used for garments or for more decorative purposes. And thus again, we are back to intent. If the cloth works well within the intended use, it may be called valid cloth.

Sett for Shadow Weave

The parameter in weaving that will always require attention for every project is sett. If the sett is correct, the beat and the selvages occur easily and in good order. The best approach for shadow weave is to start with the recommended sett for plain weave. Successful setts for specific yarns are found in the table in appendix A.

Distinction between Rising and Sinking Shed Tie-Ups

Today there are more jack looms in use than other types, and, as we know, jack looms function as rising shed looms. Counterbalance looms function as sinking shed looms. It is important to know whether the tie-up in any given draft is indicated as a rising shed tie-up or a sinking shed tie-up. Most of the time the draft source will tell you which is used.

Atwater generally gave both types of tie-ups in her publications, although she wove mainly with a rising shed loom. In Powell's book on shadow weave she gives both types of tie-ups as well; however, she says the drafts in the book use sinking shed tie-ups.

Switching from rising shed tie-ups to sinking shed tie-ups involves a simple step. If you begin with a rising shed tie-up and would like to switch to a sinking shed tie-up, merely tie the treadles where there are blank spaces instead of using the dark spaces.

The drafts in this book use the rising shed tie-up, primarily.

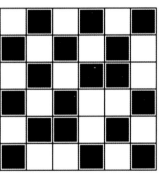

Rising-shed six-shaft Powell method tie-up

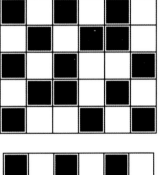

Sinking-shed six-shaft Powell method tie-up

In shadow weave the cloth is reversible, but it's not the same on the reverse. When using weaving software there are several pathways for managing how you view the two sides of the cloth on your electronic device. These may be called by various names, depending on the software. One pathway consists of merely inverting the tie-up as we have done for the rising and sinking shed tie-ups. Another is a setting or option that tells the software whether you are using a rising or sinking shed loom. A third pathway is the viewing of the front or the back of the cloth. If you combine permutations of a couple of these pathways, your drawdown view will change. The point here is to be aware of how your software works. If you are, then you can determine how you would like to view your drafts. In any case, when you take yarn to loom, you will still have cloth that is reversible and is not the same on the reverse.

Below are two drafts to demonstrate inverted tie-ups. These drafts illustrate the two sides of the same cloth. Note there are changes in the color of the featherstitching and changes in the direction of the hatching.

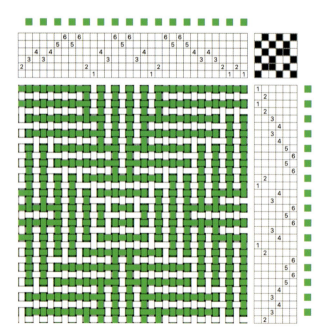

Full Draft using the rising-shed six-shaft Powell method tie-up

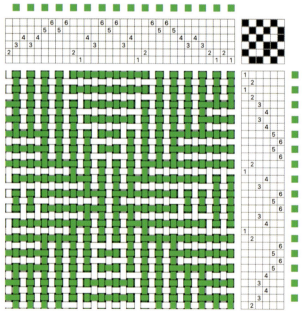

Full draft using the sinking-shed six-shaft Powell method tie-up

Management of Selvages

In shadow weave, some attention to the management of the selvages will improve the appearance of the weaving. Because of the structure of shadow weave, the two-thread floats move in and out of the selvages, alternating there with plain weave. The outermost selvage end may remain uncaught by weft in some parts of the weave.

The most common type of selvage management for shadow weave is the use of a floating selvage. Many weavers are familiar with its use, and it works well to create a fairly even edge.

There is another method to consider. It consists of wrapping or linking the two wefts together at the edges in a manner that always encircles the outermost warp end. One student called this making a "pinkie swear" with the two weft threads. This is a perfect description.

Those who are familiar with the log cabin weave will understand this concept. Similar to shadow weave, for log cabin the light threads and the dark threads alternate in the weft. We must interlock the two wefts when they emerge from the same selvage side to ensure the edge warp end is always encircled.

This is accomplished in log cabin by consistent placement of the two shuttles. For example, the first shuttle may need to be placed consistently nearer to the weaver, in relation to the second shuttle. This would be done each time the shuttles are switched to weave the next pick. However, because of the structure of shadow weave and how it works at the selvages, the weaver cannot gain any benefit from consistent placement of the shuttles to ensure the wefts wrap around the edge warp threads.

Essentially, the second method involves *reading* what is happening at the edge, and responding accordingly. We only need to read the edge with every other pick when both threads are emerging from the same side. As with anything else, it just takes a little bit of practice for weaving to progress smoothly with this method.

There are three different edge configurations to note and recognize.

1. (a) Here we see both dark and light emerging **over** the top of the edge warp. Management here is easy, since either weft going into the shed will encircle the edge warp thread.

1. (b) This situation is basically the same as 1. (a), with both dark and light emerging from **underneath** the edge warp. Management is the same as for 1. (a).

2. Here we see the light weft emerging from under the edge warp thread, and the dark is over the top of the edge warp thread. As shown, the light weft must be placed over the dark weft. This interlocking of the two wefts encircles the edge warp thread.

3. Here we see the light weft emerging over the top of the edge warp thread, and the dark is under the edge warp thread. As shown, the light weft must be placed under the dark weft to interlock and encircle the edge warp thread.

In this picture we see how the weft locks into place around the outermost warp end, as for the third situation. There is no need to touch or handle the selvages. Read the edge, note the required response, and allow the shuttles to do their work.

The color order in all of these illustrations is arbitrary. Whatever the color, dark or light, the management at the edge would be the same, depending on how the wefts are emerging from that side.

Any method of edge management in shadow weave creates selvages that are consistently inconsistent, which in and of itself is a kind of consistency. In the picture below, we have cloth that has been wet-finished. It is 3/2 cotton, so you can see more clearly the results of the method described.

Finished selvage edge

No Possible Plain Weave in Atwater or Powell Shadow Weave

In Atwater or Powell shadow weave there is no possibility of weaving a true plain weave. Take a look at the Powell Method color draft. It has a point twill fashion threading. The unit treadlings were repeated in an attempt to find a plain weave. As we can see in the structure draft, none of the usual treadlings produced a plain weave across the entire width of the cloth. The first two treadles are likely possible treadlings for plain weave, since they are tied in the usual plain weave configuration. However, we find a two-thread float in this draft where the warp is threaded with ends on 2 and 6 together. As we know, we must have an odd/even sequence for true plain weave. All the remaining treadles create two-thread floats as well.

CHAPTER 3 Basic Design Considerations

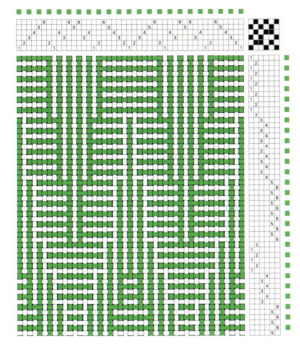

Powell Method Color Draft

Powell Method Structure Draft

A word of caution. When weaving with any of the treadle pairs as we have done in this draft, we have a rib with two warp ends running inside weft floats on the front and on the reverse. Using two treadles repeatedly may be an option to use for weaving hems of towels, for example. If the two ends are dented in the same dent, they are free to wind over one another inside the rib that is created. Since you have one dark and one light weaving inside that rib, it appears in the cloth as a major error. There are two light threads occurring side by side, and two darks as well. When this happens, it is glaring.

The solution is to separate the ends into different dents. Paying attention to this as you weave saves you a little handwork later, when you may like to slide the errant ends back into place by hand with a needle. When there is only one end per dent, this aberration occurs less easily. As you begin to treadle the rest of your shadow weave pattern, these two ends behave very well and fall back into their appropriate place.

Notice the vertical stripes on either side of the lower central motif in this sample. It appears as a possible planned motif. However, the vertical stripes in question should appear as the two motifs on the sides.

47

Parallel Shadow Weave

There is one other system of managing shadow weave that does create a plain weave. It is called parallel shadow weave, devised by Elizabeth Lang and Erica Dakin Voolich. In this method, twice as many shafts are required to achieve the designs, and multiple shaft weavers may wish to pursue it further. Because we are limiting the information in this book to eight shafts or fewer, this method will not be addressed. Parallel shadow weave does offer a third way of drafting that creates the exact same cloth that can be woven with the Atwater and the Powell methods on fewer shafts. Take a look at appendix C for an example.

Extended Twill

Understanding the basic concept of extended twill is important, and here is a basic definition to lay a foundation. Extended twill may be defined simply as the name suggests—it is a continuation of the twill line. A six-shaft straight twill is threaded 1, 2, 3, 4, 5, 6. To extend it we would merely start over and thread 1 through 6 again.

A six-shaft regular point twill would be threaded 1 through 6 and then back down to 1. If we wanted to extend the point twill, we would thread this entire point, then we would thread from 6 to 1 again, which can be repeated as desired. We can extend point twill in either direction by repeating the straight twill lines of the point, and by following the slant of the twill lines. The extended-twill draft offers an example.

The draft is as drawn in, with two repeats in both the threading and the treadling. Also note, this draft illustrates the importance of viewing multiple repeats of any draft. You will find some wonderful motifs created at the joining of the repeats. This is true in shadow weave as well.

Extending a shadow weave draft is a little trickier. First you will need to understand more about how shadow weave works.

Regular six-shaft extended-point-twill draft

CHAPTER 4

Designing Shadow Weave with the Atwater Method

How to Draft Shadow Weave with the Atwater Method

Mary Meigs Atwater developed shadow weave on a parallel threading and treadling draft. Just where and when the name "parallel" came into existence related to weaving is not clear from references. Parallel-weave drafting is widely used. The popular echo weave uses such a draft. We also find the term "parallel" as a function within most weaving software. With only a couple of clicks of the computer mouse, we can create a parallel threading and treadling draft.

The steps for creating an Atwater method shadow weave draft with the parallel threading are as follows:

1. For an eight-shaft draft, write or enter a desired twill line on every other square of your grid. Make these first ends dark, and as such they are considered by Atwater to be the dominant or controlling ends.

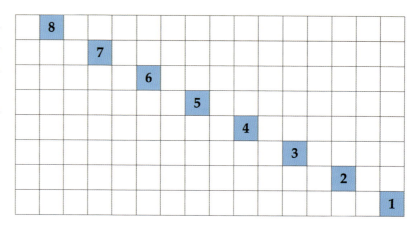

2. Then write or enter another twill line in the squares between those added in step 1. They will be written onto the draft a predetermined number of shafts or rows away from the first twill line. The distance between the twill lines is half the number of shafts available. In this case we will add them four shafts from the first twill line. Make these the "shadowing" ends, which historically are light ends.

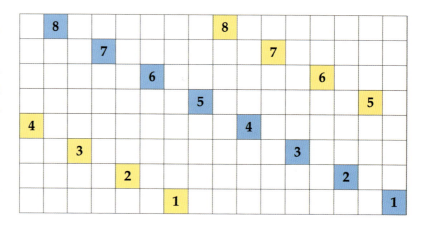

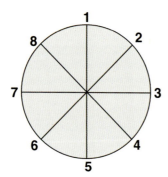

3. For the parallel twill lines we just created in step 2, we may refer to the twill circle for eight shafts to find where the light ends go on the draft. We started our draft at 1. We then skip directly across the circle to find 5, which is four steps around the circle from 1. Then we find 6 across from 2, and so on around the circle. When we get to 5 in our basic twill line, we again move across the circle and place the shadowing end on 1. Then we continue around the circle to create the remainder of the parallel threading. We also call this type of draft "on opposites," which is illustrated aptly by the twill circle.

We now have one repeat of an eight-shaft, parallel, straight-twill fashion shadow weave threading. In the graphic we can easily see why it is called parallel threading.

Of course, we can create an "on opposites" parallel threading on four or six shafts as well, using their respective twill circles, as shown. The shadowing ends are two steps from the dark dominant on four shafts, and three steps from the dark dominant on six shafts.

The drafts we just created are unidirectional, meaning the twill lines do not make reversals or points.

It is important to note that the choice of dark or light in this manner is arbitrary, and the value of the ends could just as easily be switched. The threads could also be different colors or hues. The key principle is that the color-and-weave effect occurs best if there is some value contrast between the two.

On the other hand, we may wish to keep our dark dominant as we move into considering shadow weave within "Block Theory" in chapter 6. We will see this as an advantage, because within the Powell method the dark dominant defines the units used to create full drafts from profiles.

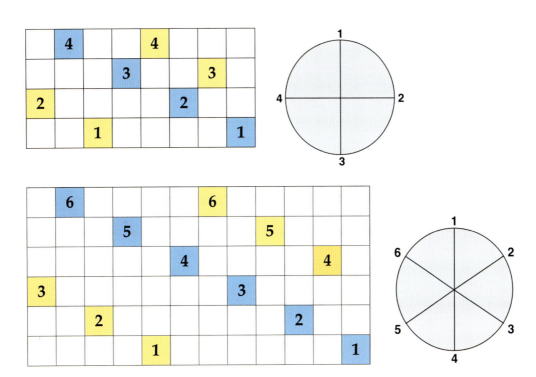

The Enigma of Shadow Weave Illuminated

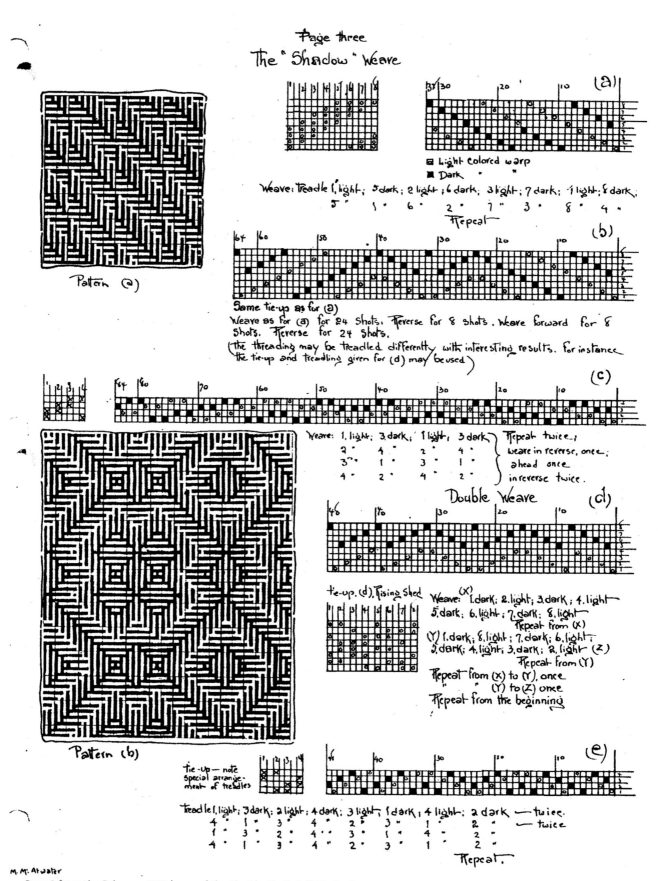

Page 3 from the February 1942 issue of the *Shuttle-Craft Guild Bulletin*

CHAPTER 4 Designing Shadow Weave with the Atwater Method

Atwater's First Drafts from the *Shuttle-Craft Guild Bulletin*

As we remember, the first publication about shadow weave was in the February 1942 issue of the *Shuttle-Craft Guild Bulletin*. Atwater named the drafts in this issue of her bulletin (a), (b), (c), (d), and (e). The interpretation of Atwater's drafts takes a bit of study because the method of indicating drafts was different in her era than those we are familiar with today. The tie-ups and threadings are given on hand-drawn grid diagrams, and the treadlings are given in sentence form.

We first see the eight-shaft tie-up at the top of the page. This is a balanced 4/4 twill tie-up. There are four shafts working opposite the other four. On a rising shed loom with eight shafts, four shafts are raised and four remain down. Then the next treadle steps up one shaft, and the rest follow in consecutive order. She indicates this is the tie-up for both (a) and (b.)

Draft (a)

The threading for (a) is shown next, illustrated on a hand-drawn grid. We find something similar to our Atwater method, straight-twill fashion shadow weave designed previously. However, in this draft Atwater added a break in the twill line of the threading. We can see the break in the center where shafts 4 and 5 are consecutive.

The treadling, as was common in 1942, is written in a text format. It is different than the threading in this draft, which is the case in quite a few of Atwater's drafts. Because of the little break in the sequence of the threading, the color-and-weave effect of this draft is consistent with the appearance of a broken twill. The full draft is interpreted in the color draft below. We would call this a broken-twill fashion draft.

This draft is unidirectional, because there are no reversals in the threading or the treadling. The woven cloth is shown on page 50.

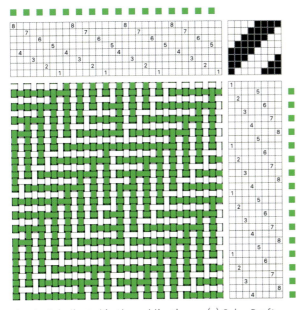

The draft indicated in the publication as (a) Color Draft

Structure draft

55

Draft (b)

Atwater's threading for (b) is also illustrated in a hand-drawn grid. For this draft she has added some points or reversals. As mentioned, Atwater indicates that the tie-up for (b) is the same as for (a). The treadling is again written in text format. When we enter this draft into our electronic software, we find there are areas of long floats. Some of these floats extend over as many as eleven threads. These are seen vertically in the center and at the sides of the draft. The long floats in this draft do not fit neatly within our definition of shadow weave, which tells us we normally have floats over two threads.

Comparing this draft with a draft of the reverse of the cloth, accomplished easily in the software by inverting the tie-up, gives us more information. Here again we find the longer floats contained within the center channel-like area, created by the three-thread floats in the weft. The structure draft shows this more clearly.

The draft indicated in the publication as (b) The As Written

CHAPTER 4 Designing Shadow Weave with the Atwater Method

The draft indicated in the publication as (b) Reverse of the As Written Draft

The Enigma of Shadow Weave Illuminated

The draft indicated in the publication as (b) As Written Structure Draft

The longer floats through the center are created because of the way Atwater managed the points. We need to remember this design represents some of the first designing of shadow weave. As the weave evolved, other methods of making adjustments at the points were devised.

CHAPTER 4 Designing Shadow Weave with the Atwater Method

The woven cloth for Atwater's draft (b) As Written

In the woven cloth, we see the long floats created in the center of each repeat of the threading. They are also seen at the edges of the repeats. The structure of the cloth is solid, and the long floats do not create any characteristic that would decrease the validity of the cloth. There is also an interesting overall diamond motif created where the threading and treadling repeats join.

Also on page 3 of the February 1942 *Shuttle-Craft Guild Bulletin* issue, Atwater included a drawdown illustration, which she labeled as "Pattern (b)." It is a wonderful example of Atwater's incredible hand-drawn illustrations found in many of her publications.

Detail illustration of Pattern (b) from the *Shuttle-Craft Guild Bulletin*

Here we find a bit of a discrepancy. The illustration does not look like the draft devised from the written instructions for (b). If only we could have had a conversation with Atwater to resolve the discrepancy. She certainly would have set us on the right path with her straightforward approach. In lieu of that, we can devise a draft more consistent with the illustration. We will call the first draft "As Written." The second draft will be called the "Illustration." This draft represents one threading and treadling repeat of the design.

Changes made to the original "As Written" draft to create the "Illustration" draft include the following:

- The points in the threading at the beginning of the repeat and the center now pivot on 1, instead of on 8.
- The treadling twill line slants in the opposite direction.
- All the treadling points pivot on 1.
- The treadling colorway was switched, dark for light and light for dark.
- In order to match the colorway of the featherstitching and the direction of the hatching, the tie-up was inverted.

CHAPTER 4 Designing Shadow Weave with the Atwater Method

The draft indicated in the publication as (b) Illustration Color Draft

The threading colorway was maintained. Also, we may note that this draft again is not as drawn in, and there remain some three-end floats. However, the long channeled floats in the center of the cloth have been eliminated. This draft does successfully match the "Illustration."

By expanding the single repeat of this draft, we can devise a draft of the full illustration called "Pattern (b)."

The cloth woven from the "Illustration" draft is very solid and durable. The plain weave hatching and the dark and light lines of the featherstitching are the prominent characteristics. This draft is shown on page 63.

61

The Enigma of Shadow Weave Illuminated

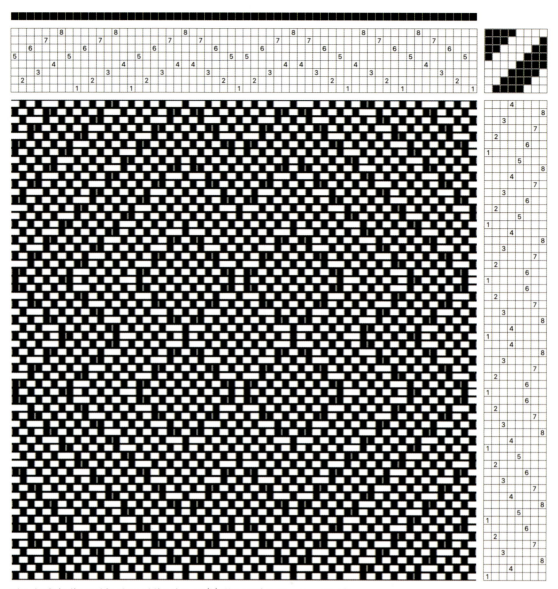

The draft indicated in the publication as (b) Illustration Structure Draft

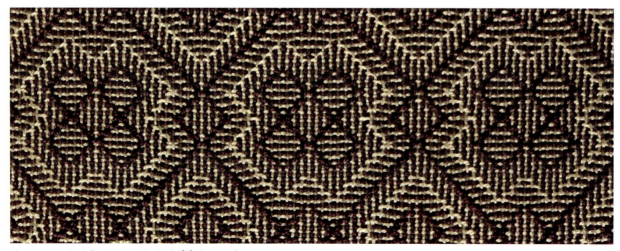

The woven cloth for Atwater's draft (b) Illustration

CHAPTER 4 Designing Shadow Weave with the Atwater Method

The draft above was created to exactly match the full illustration for "Pattern (b)."

63

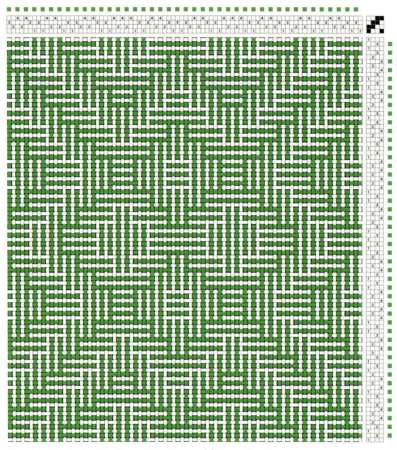

The draft indicated in the publication as (c) Color Draft

Draft (c)

Atwater usually included four-shaft drafts in her publications for those who had looms with fewer shafts. This article is no exception.

The treadling was a bit of a challenge for me to determine for (c). The difficulty occurs when encountering the points or reversals in the draft, and it was a challenge to determine on which thread to pivot. The draft for (c) represents one interpretation of the instructions.

The patterning motif in (c) is similar to the (b) Illustration draft, and Atwater says on page 2, "Draft (c) is a four harness version . . . of the figure at draft (b)." It has less distinctive lines, which are created in a stairstepping manner. There is a softer look to the overall patterning.

There certainly is an optical shimmer when looking at this structure draft on the printed page.

Interestingly, the weaving of this sample was more of a challenge than the previous samples. One would think it would be easier to weave four-shaft shadow weave, but the threading and the treadling were much less intuitive than those on eight shafts. The weaving required following the treadling sequence pick by pick. This difficulty is due to the nature of four-shaft extended twill, in that the twill wraps back more frequently to the beginning of the twill line.

Also, it is more difficult to see the surface patterning at the loom. This is due to the two-thread floats being closer together, which also means there are smaller areas of hatching. The landmarks that give us a visual pathway are much less distinctive in this four-shaft weave. From this experience, we may conclude it is more difficult to weave four-shaft shadow weave than it is to weave six- or eight-shaft shadow weave. This draft certainly offers an intricate type of cloth to weave on a loom with fewer shafts.

CHAPTER 4 Designing Shadow Weave with the Atwater Method

The draft indicated in the publication as (c) Structure Draft

The woven cloth for Atwater's draft (c)

65

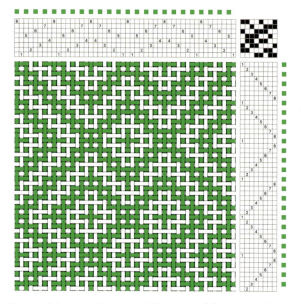

The draft indicated in the publication as (d) Color Draft

Structure draft

Draft (d)

Atwater's discussion in her article for drafts (d) and (e) is as follows:

> Draft (d), also warped in two colors and woven in two colors, produces a figure similar to (b) in a true doubleweave. And, believe it or not, so does the four-harness version at (e)—though the eight-harness effect is a bit neater and sharper in effect than the four-harness weave. *(page 2)*

She also labels the (d) draft as "Double Weave" in bold lettering above it on page 3. We again see the threading and the tie-up represented in handwritten grids, which are easily transferred to electronic drafts. Note the tie-up is very different than the previous drafts. The instructions for the treadling (d) are written in text format.

It is curious that the treadling contains straight lines of twill, while the threading is parallel. There's another question to add to our topics of discussion with Atwater, should we ever meet. How did she derive this draft? It is also interesting to note that the structure draft shows there is no plain weave, and it appears as a twill configuration.

When we work with doubleweave in electronic drafts, or on paper, for that matter, we soon learn we cannot really see the whole picture of the cloth in our two-dimensional processes. This is true of shadow weave as well. It is certainly a challenge to represent three-dimensional designs accurately in a two-dimensional format.

The draft on the opposite page represents two repeats of draft (d). It has a surface patterning that looks like the "Pattern (b)" illustration.

An aspect to examine in this draft is the way the dark and the light floats occur; a square configuration can be seen. The little squares are made of two rows of floats reminiscent of the shadow weave featherstitching. This cloth is reversible, and where there is dark on one side, it is light on the other.

CHAPTER 4 Designing Shadow Weave with the Atwater Method

Two repeats of the draft indicated in the publication as (d)

67

The doubleweave occurs in narrow diagonal channels. The photo at the right shows the cloth on the loom as it was being woven. The structure was a little more easily seen at the loom in a fully tensioned warp, versus after the sample was wet-finished.

Since this is doubleweave, a closer sett was required than for the other drafts. This cloth is solid. It does have quite a bit of give and stretchability when pulled on the bias. However, this does not detract from the validity of the cloth. It is a very interesting draft and cloth to consider.

The woven cloth for Atwater's draft (d) on the loom

The finished woven cloth for Atwater's draft (d)

Draft (e)

Atwater also calls the four-shaft draft (e) "Double Weave." The draft for the four-shaft Double Weave appears very reminiscent of shadow weave, with the same feather-stitching-style design lines. In the actual cloth we see that the dark and the light diagonal lines appear exactly as the featherstitching is described earlier. There is no plain weave apparent in the cloth between these lines. However, we can see some very narrow lines of single-thread floats in the structure draft. The sample was woven at a sett of 20 epi, also in 5/2 cotton.

The motif is the same in all these drafts from the 1942 article, and Atwater says she designed the drafts, especially the doubleweave drafts, from a photograph of a sixteen-shaft "ancient piece." The photograph was not published with the article. She goes on to say the four- and eight-shaft versions are not quite as elaborate as the sixteen-shaft cloth in the photo, and she was surprised to find it could be woven at all on four shafts.

Enjoy these Atwater method drafts, which have not been available for many years. Finding this issue of the *Shuttle-Craft Guild Bulletin* represented a challenge, since it did not exist online during the time I was researching. It was listed in the bibliography of Powell's book and was obtained through the generosity of our weaving community. Now, through the wonderful generosity of the Mary Meigs Atwater Weaver's Guild of Utah, all of the *Shuttle-Craft Guild Bulletins* are available and may be found on their website.

And another enduring question remains about all of the Atwater samples—"How long has it been since anyone has woven something using these drafts?"

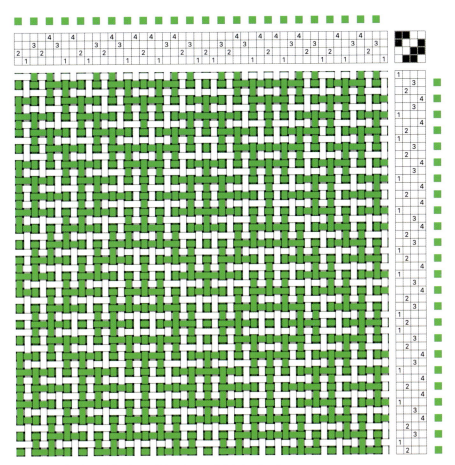

The draft indicated in the publication as (e) Color Draft

The Enigma of Shadow Weave Illuminated

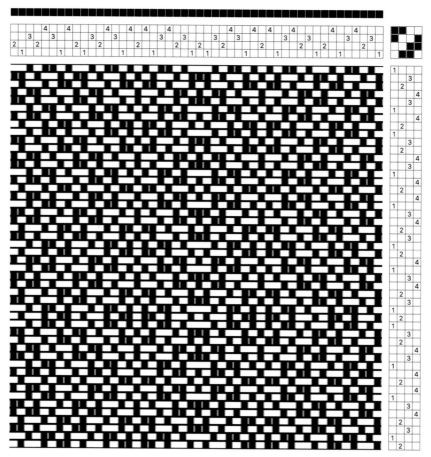

Structure draft

CHAPTER 4 Designing Shadow Weave with the Atwater Method

The woven cloth for Atwater's draft (e)

CHAPTER 5

Powell Conversion and Drafting

◇◇

In a March 1960 article in *Shuttle Craft*, Powell presented her "Shadow Weave Conversion." She said she needed to weave some "last-minute Christmas sport jacket yardage," and she wanted to find an easier way to weave an Atwater shadow weave draft, given her time limitations. The conversion produces a draft that has a straight twill line. She deemed this much easier to thread and treadle.

Before we discuss the actual conversion Powell devised, let us consider a little historical background. Powell and the weavers of her time wrote drafts by hand on "point paper," otherwise known as graph paper. This consisted of writing out, on blank graph paper, the entire weaving draft. This may be a good exercise for all weavers to complete at some time in their weaving career for a real hands-on understanding of how weaving interlacements occur. First you write in the threading and the treadling, and then the tie-up. The drawdown is added last, by coloring in where the warp and weft interlace with over and under floats. The drawdown, as we know, represents the actual cloth created by the draft.

Powell used several different strips of graph paper to help create her drawdowns. Each one was a single row of squares, and they were made by coloring in the squares for each individual line of the design in the draft drawdown. The strips were positioned next to the appropriate line on the new draft, and the design was copied. Powell recommends using these templates in her book.

Powell treadling sample

If you would like to complete the conversion on paper in the spirit of Powell's methods, create the drafts in your own software or on graph paper. You will be cutting narrow strips for each shaft and each treadle, so print your drafts as large as you are able. When cutting the strips, be sure to include the tieup horizontally for the shafts and vertically for the treadles. This sounds like a lot of complicated work. However, I encourage you to complete this hands-on exercise for yourself, because when I did it, I experienced one of those rare moments when the light blinked on.

In weaving software this process is made simple by using functions offered there. The principles are the same. You will be converting from a parallel threading to a regular twill fashion sequencing.

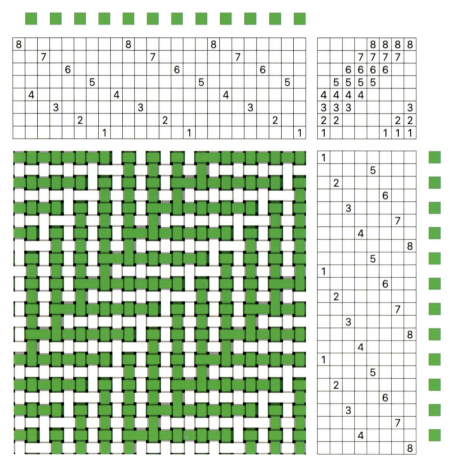

The Atwater draft

Powell Conversion Steps

For the conversion we begin with a simple as-drawn-in Atwater draft designed from a straight twill. A structure draft is included, which will be valuable to compare with the converted Powell draft.

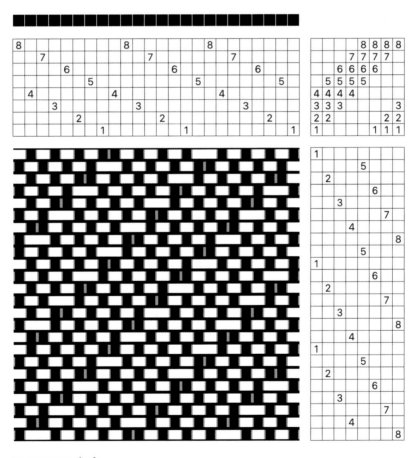

Its structure draft

The Enigma of Shadow Weave Illuminated

Powell Conversion Step 1:

Rearrange the *threading* of the shafts to make the first eight warp threads form a straight twill line from 1 through 8. *Include the tie-up* in this shifting of the shafts.

In order to create the straight-twill *threading line*, shift the shafts as follows, beginning from the right of the threading:

1. Warp on shaft 1 stays on shaft 1.
2. Warp on shaft 5, which is the next warp as we move to the left along the threading, is moved to shaft 2.
3. Warp on shaft 2 is moved to shaft 3.
4. Warp on shaft 6 is moved to shaft 4.
5. Warp on shaft 3 is moved to shaft 5.
6. Warp on shaft 7 is moved to shaft 6.
7. Warp on shaft 4 is moved to shaft 7.
8. Warp on shaft 8 stays on shaft 8.

The results of this step are shown in the next draft. The tie-up is shown unnumbered, since weaving software will not recognize the kind of shifting of numbers we are creating on paper. The numbering can be seen in the tie-up grid to the right. Also note that the second twill line of the threading appears in a different order. This will be explained a bit later.

And another result to note—the visual effect in the drawdown did not change.

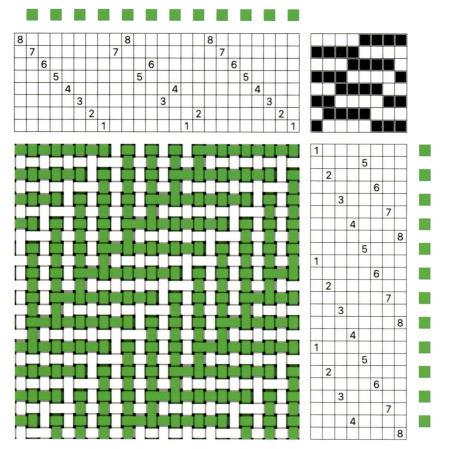

Draft resulting from the Powell conversion step 1

View of the tie-up numbering after completing step 1

Powell Conversion Step 2:

Start with the *draft created as a result of step 1*, with the oddly numbered tie-up. Rearrange the *treadling* order to make the first eight weft picks form a straight twill line from 1 through 8. *Include the tie-up* in this shifting of the treadlings.

In order to create the straight-twill *treadling line*, shift the strips as follows:

1. Weft on shaft 1 stays on treadle 1.
2. Weft on shaft 5 is moved to treadle 2.
3. Weft on shaft 2 is moved to treadle 3.
4. Weft on shaft 6 is moved to treadle 4.
5. Weft on shaft 3 is moved to treadle 5.
6. Weft on shaft 7 is moved to treadle 6.
7. Weft on shaft 4 is moved to treadle 7.
8. Weft on shaft 8 stays on treadle 8.

Now we are seeing the as-drawn-in treadling with the same twill lines. We also see a very different tie-up, which is the eight-shaft tie-up for Powell shadow weave.

The tie-up has shifted twice as we followed Powell's two-step conversion process.

The order of changes in step 2 is the same as the order of changes in step 1. Below is the final eight-shaft draft created from the Powell conversion and its accompanying structure draft. The drawdown, and therefore the resulting cloth, is exactly the same as the starting Atwater draft.

The method of converting a four- or a six-shaft draft from Atwater to Powell follows the same process. On the next page find the steps for converting these drafts. Of course, the tie-ups shift just like they do with the eight-shaft draft, to create the distinctive Powell tie-ups.

It is interesting to note that the conversion on a four-shaft draft merely consists of interchanging all ends or picks on shafts 2 and 3. The 2s go to 3, and the 3s go to 2.

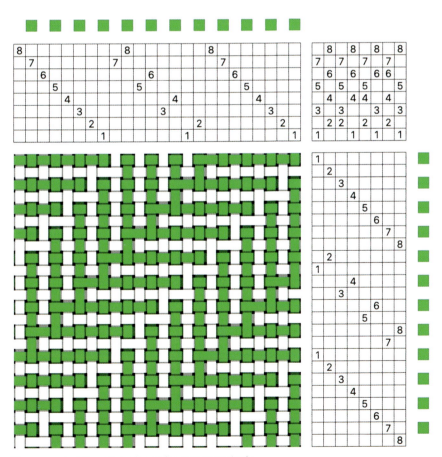

The converted Powell draft and its structure draft

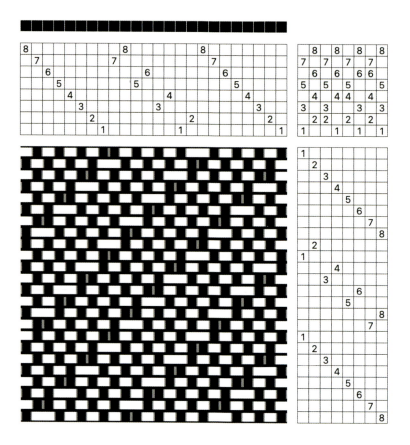

Four-Shaft Steps

1. Warp or weft on 1 stays on 1.
2. Warp or weft on 3 is moved to 2.
3. Warp or weft on 2 is moved to 3.
4. Warp or weft on 4 stays on 4.

Six-Shaft Steps

1. Warp or weft on 1 stays on 1.
2. Warp or weft on 4 is moved to 2.
3. Warp or weft on 2 is moved to 3.
4. Warp or weft on 5 is moved to 4.
5. Warp or weft on 3 is moved to 5.
6. Warp or weft on 6 stays on 6.

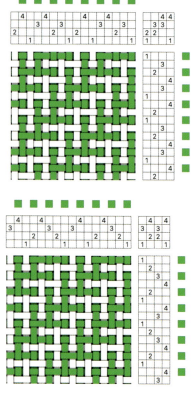

The four-shaft Atwater draft is at top, and the Powell is below it.

CHAPTER 5 Powell Conversion and Drafting

In Powell shadow weave the tie-ups are standard. Below are tie-ups for four-, six-, and eight-shaft drafts for rising shed looms.

Marian Powell devised many drafts using her conversion. One excellent learning exercise would be to plan and weave a sample warp of multiple treadlings for a single threading. The best place to learn about shadow weave is at the loom. After we delve into a few more aspects of Powell's methods and approach in chapter 6, follow her lead and create your own shadow weave drafts.

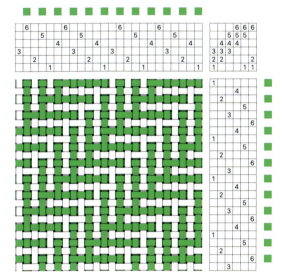
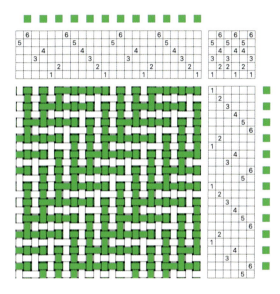

The six-shaft Atwater draft is above, and the Powell is on the right.

Powell shadow weave tie-ups

79

CHAPTER 6

Block Theory and Shadow Weave

◇◇◇

Marian Powell developed her many drafts for weaving samples by using profile drafts. Defining terms and concepts related to profile drafts and block weaves will help us understand how she worked with shadow weave.

Summer & winter is a very common example of a block or unit weave. When we examine the cloth, we see there are areas we would call pattern and areas we would call background. The areas with longer weft floats are commonly designated as the pattern, and the areas where we see more of the plain weave ground cloth are the background. Most block weaves have these two distinctive areas of pattern and background, and when we are designing block weaves, they are an important consideration.

Summer & winter cloth

Shadow weave does not have these separate and distinct pattern and background areas. This is true unless we designate the two different hatching areas as such. At the beginning of Powell's narrative in her book on page 3, she says, "As the eye moves more readily in a horizontal than vertical line, the horizontal pin stripes will be considered positive, vertical stripes negative" (1976). This means she designated the horizontal hatching as the pattern, and the vertical hatching as the background.

Profile Drafts

A profile draft is merely a visual representation of a pattern or design. We write them in a gridded format, similar to our full weaving drafts, with what appear to be the four basic components—the threading, the tie-up, the treadling, and the drawdown. While we may use this draft format for profiles, it is only a shorthand for the actual full draft. We will add specific threadings and treadlings into individual squares on the profile draft. Each weave structure has its own code, key, or "unit" to insert into the squares, which would give us the full draft.

Historically, and in many of the older references, the profile draft was called a "short draft." When considering the task of handwriting drafts, using short drafts would not take as much time to hand-draw the resulting patterning created in the cloth.

For the discussion about profile drafts, I will keep the quotation marks around some of the words. This may be one of the most challenging topics to speak about in weaving, because we use the same words for the sections of two different visual graphics. One graphic is the profile draft, and the other is the full weaving draft. The quotes are used when I am speaking about the sections of the profile draft. My hope is that this will assist you to conceptualize these concepts. We also use the terms "block" and "unit" interchangeably, which is not accurate, although they are related. The "block" is the design, and the "unit" is the key that leads us to our chosen weave structure.

I will reiterate the point—in a profile draft we call the squares of the grid "blocks" when referring to the *design*. The lower row of squares in the "threading" area would contain the "A" blocks. The next row above block A contains the "B" blocks, and so on. The same convention applies to the "treadling" section, with the left column as block "A." The next column to the right would be block "B." These squares or blocks then create the visual design we are working to obtain in the "drawdown" portion of our profile draft.

Some weave structures have *exact* codes, keys, or "units" to insert into the profile draft. A good example of this is four-shaft summer & winter. The unit code for what we call block A in summer & winter is threaded and treadled 1, 3, 2, 3. All four of these actual warp ends or weft picks are added into the draft for each A block square on the profile. Blocks B, C, and D each have their own distinct unit code. Once you know the code, you are off and weaving. This is called a "unit weave," and for these there are no exceptions or incidentals to consider. Straight-twill fashion and asymmetrical shadow weave fall into this category because drafts for these can also be devised directly from the exact unit codes.

A design block is also a vertical column in the "drawdown" where we see the design created in the "cloth." The unit squares can be repeated in the profile "threading" and "treadling" grids to create the desired width or length of the design. These repeated units together become a "block" or a design in the "drawdown." When the "A" block vertical column intersects with the "A" block horizontal rows, and we have the "A" block in the tie-up, we get a black block of design in the "drawdown" of our profile. This is true because we assume our profile "warp" is black and our "weft" is white. Refer to the Six-Block Profile Draft to see this concept clearly.

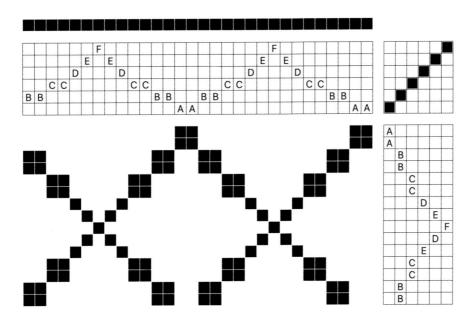

Six-block profile draft

Atwater Shadow Weave Units

Before going further, we need to define the shadow weave unit designations for the Atwater and the Powell methods. Take a look at them in the two graphics. Included are the colorways of dark and light. The darks are highlighted in green and underlined. The lights are not highlighted, and they are not underlined.

The Atwater method is not necessarily considered a block weave, and because of this we would not normally assign units. However, delineating the units for Atwater, as well as Powell, offers an opportunity to compare. Take a moment to absorb the information offered in these graphics to see the difference between the Atwater and Powell methods. Atwater shows the parallel threading, on opposites. Also notice the units are not the same for four, six, and eight shafts.

Six-shaft units are included here for several reasons. There are some really wonderful six-shaft drafts available, and Powell included six-shaft drafts in her book, along with the four and eight. Also, there was a time when six-shaft looms were manufactured. This is an area that weavers could explore more fully. Six-shaft shadow weave creates a step between the more overall designs made on four shafts, and provides a daintier option than seen in the bold cloth made on eight.

	Atwater Method Units		
Design block	**4-shaft units**	**6-shaft units**	**8-shaft units**
Block A	_1_ 3	_1_ 4	_1_ 5
Block B	_2_ 4	_2_ 5	_2_ 6
Block C	_3_ 1	_3_ 6	_3_ 7
Block D	_4_ 2	_4_ 1	_4_ 8
Block E	– –	_5_ 2	_5_ 1
Block F	– –	_6_ 3	_6_ 2
Block G	– –	– –	_7_ 3
Block H	– –	– –	_8_ 4

In this material:

Dark threads on a numbered shaft or treadle appear in this way: **_1_**

Light threads on a numbered shaft or treadle appear in this way: 2

Powell Shadow Weave Units

The Powell units show the sequential twill fashion lines. The first four units create a numbering from 1 through 8 when we include both the dark and the light of the unit pairs. The unit for block A is **1**-2, B is **3**-4, C is **5**-6, and D is **7**-8. This would be our first eight-shaft, straight-twill fashion line as created in the Powell conversion.

We also created another twill line that does not make a consecutively numbered straight run. If using an accurate descriptor, we could call this second twill line the "second set" of units. These units take into consideration the color-and-weave definition, which is the combining of the colorway with the structure. If we have a unit with dark on **1** and light on 2, then we must also have the opposite, which is dark on **2** and light on 1. This is how we create a complete complement of combinations. In the graphic the units in the second set are seen below the red line.

Here again, the units are not the same for four, six, and eight shafts. We have also discovered there are as many units as there are shafts.

These are the block units Powell used to create the drafts in her book. She included a similar list, which she calls the "Magic Key." I have found that with students, when the information about profile drafts clicks with them, a whole other world within weaving opens for them. I would agree this is a magical moment.

	Powell Method Units		
Design block	**4-shaft units**	**6-shaft units**	**8-shaft units**
Block A	**1** 2	**1** 2	**1** 2
Block B	**3** 4	**3** 4	**3** 4
Block C	**2** 1	**5** 6	**5** 6
Block D	**4** 3	**2** 1	**7** 8
Block E	– –	**4** 3	**2** 1
Block F	– –	**6** 5	**4** 3
Block G	– –	– –	**6** 5
Block H	– –	– –	**8** 7

A Unidirectional Draft

In a unidirectional draft the direction of the twill fashion line slants in one direction, meaning there are no points or reversals. The units are used exactly with no adjustments needed, and therefore this draft is a unit weave.

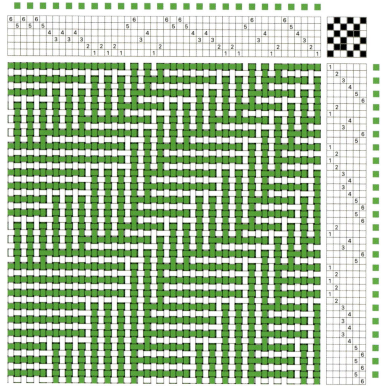

Unidirectional draft

Symmetrical Drafts and Point Twill Fashion Adjustments

There are some block weave structures, such as overshot or crackle, that require adjustments to the threading and treadling after inserting the unit code. If we do not make the adjustments, the result may include very long floats or other aberrations in our cloth. In various references the adjustments are also called "exceptions" or "incidentals." These types of weave structures are "nonunit" weaves.

Most of the drafts in Powell's book contain balanced diamonds, ovals, rectangles, or other interesting motifs outlined with dark or light featherstitching. They are pleasing designs, since we can easily interpret the motifs found in the cloth. "Symmetrical" is an apt name for these designs. We also find that the threading and treadling used to create the designs in cloth are symmetrical. Therefore, we will also call the weaving drafts "symmetrical."

Symmetrical point twill fashion shadow weave is considered a nonunit weave because adjustments need to be made where there are reversals or points in the twill lines to make the visual patterning in the cloth symmetrical. Powell called the symmetrical drafts "preferred" because the distinctive diagonal featherstitching lines are maintained.

Using the term "reversal" is also apt. It means there is a change in direction of the twill line. When we refer again to the twill circles in chapter 4, we see a reversal occurs when we go back the other direction around the circle.

Shared Units

Now let's take a step back and look at a regular point twill draft on six shafts. When we count from the thread on 1 up to 6 and back down to include 1, we discover there are an odd number of ends in a single point threading—for this draft it is eleven ends. This would be one full point if it stood by itself. We can also see the three ends circled at the points in the draft—also an odd number.

As we remember, our shadow weave units each consist of two threads. When the units are taken singly or combined in any manner, they would consist of an even number of threads. This factor creates a problem when designing all the wonderful point twill fashion, symmetrical shadow weave designs, which have an odd number of ends at the point. We solve this problem by making adjustments to our draft at the points or reversals.

Basically, we either add *or* subtract one end or pick at the reversals. Our goal is to always have an odd number of ends or picks at the reversals in our symmetrical drafts, just like we have in the regular point twill draft. Powell generally adds one end in her book.

The next concept to consider, then, is that some of the threads at the points in shadow weave will be shared by two units. In the next draft we see there are three ends circled on two of the points in the threading. Look at the ends circled on shafts 1 and 2. If we read those circled ends from the right, the first unit is light on 2 and dark on 1. The second unit is dark on 1 and light on 2. The single end on 1 is shared by the two units. This also occurs with the end circled on 5. The shared threads occur in both the threading and the treadling, as ends or picks.

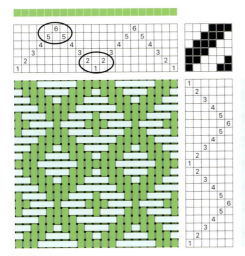

Regular six-shaft point-twill draft

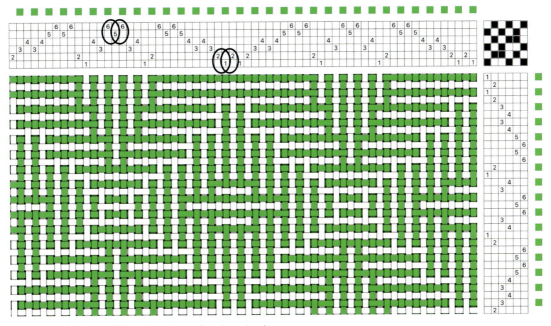

Symmetrical point-twill fashion draft with shared units

Tidball supports this rule for managing the reversals. She says the following in the July 1953 *Shuttle Craft Guild Handweaver's Bulletin*, on page 4: "Just as in Point twill drafts or Overshot drafts, an odd number of threads must occur in the reverse unit."

The simple six-block profile draft, which was developed from the shadow weave draft on page 87, is shown below. If we go back to our units list for the Powell method, we can see how the full draft was developed from this profile. The parameters for making the adjustments at the points were also followed when creating the full draft. Compare the overall design seen in the drawdown of the profile to the full draft with the shadow weave structure created. The "A" blocks were not repeated at the end of the threading and the treadling areas, because they will appear as a pivot point when repeating the draft.

Here is a question to ponder. If we have shared units at the reversals, should we have one block unit at the reversals of this profile draft? Or should we have two?

The answer: **The profile draft is just a tool for designing. It is up to the designer as to how they wish to use it.**

The bottom draft on this page is another example of a symmetrical draft that has an odd number of ends at the reversal or point. We can see the units are repeated to give a wider area of design. The symmetry is maintained if we also maintain the odd number of ends at the point, even if we repeat the unit many times. The treadling in this draft is unidirectional.

Of course the Atwater draft requires the same adjustments at the reversals to maintain symmetry. On the facing page (top) is the same draft converted back to the Atwater method. There are an odd number of ends at the point in this draft as well.

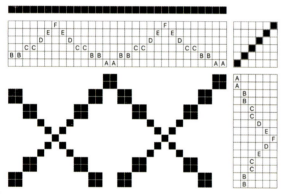

Six-block profile draft

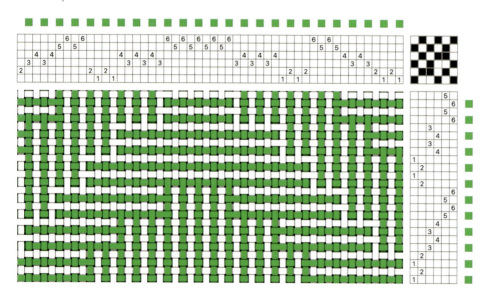

Powell method draft with units repeated

CHAPTER 6 Block Theory and Shadow Weave

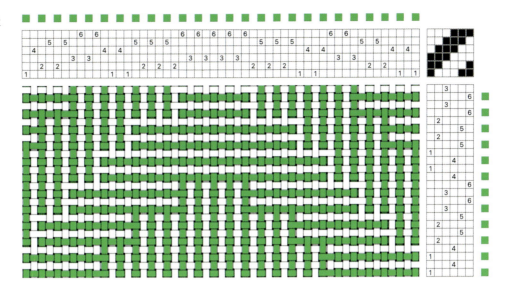

Atwater method draft with units repeated

Asymmetrical Drafts

Asymmetrical drafts, which Powell called "secondary," are also possible and are an additional design decision when drafting shadow weave. The name "asymmetrical" here refers primarily to the threading and the treadling, although we create asymmetry in the overall patterning in the drawdown as well. No adjustments are made at the reversals, and the units are used exactly. As such, this draft is a unit weave.

The design is certainly not as distinctive or clearly outlined as the symmetrical drafts. However, if we squint or look closely, we can see diamonds. The visual patterning does appear offset, and this is because the reversals or points in the threading and treadling are asymmetrical.

The featherstitching has also changed. In some areas it is distinct, with a single value or color. In other areas the diagonal featherstitching line is much less distinct.

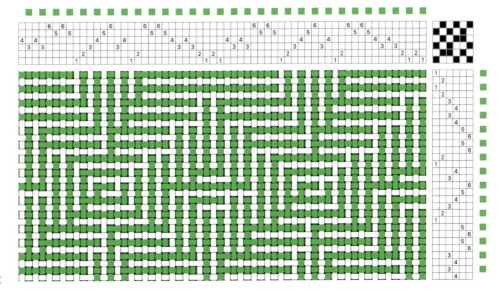

Six-shaft asymmetrical point-twill fashion draft

89

This is because the featherstitching contains one dark float and one light float. We will also find this characteristic in another design method called Switch Draft, which will be discussed in chapter 7.

Here is another draft developed as asymmetrical. Compare the draft with the woven cloth pictured on page 80. The outlining of the motifs creates a more subtle effect than we see in symmetrical shadow weave.

Eight-shaft asymmetrical draft

The Design Blocks Weave Together

Another consideration in our discussion about block theory is the fact that blocks will weave pattern at the same time in shadow weave. We examine this concept by starting with another kind of profile draft. Look at the "tie-up" portion of our profile draft to understand how this works. Weaving designers can vary what is added there, depending on the design desired. A simple profile "tie-up" has one square for each "shaft" and "treadle," which creates a single diagonal line in the "tie-up." For this "tie-up," blocks occur individually. The "A" blocks in the "threading," "treadling," and "tie-up" make corresponding individual squares of design within the "drawdown" space.

Simple four-block profile draft

For more complex designs, any other patterning the weaver chooses can be placed into the "tie-up" area. This is called a combined block profile.

The typical tie-up used for balanced 4/4 twill on eight shafts was chosen for the next profile draft. This is the tie-up used by Atwater for shadow weave. Because blocks A, B, C, and D are tied up to the first "treadle," all four of those blocks will show black pattern blocks in the "drawdown" area. We find these represented by the dark rows of horizontal design at the top of the "drawdown" in this draft. We may note these dark rows are beneath the A, B, C, and D blocks in the "threading."

Next we need to add in our units and create a thread-by-thread full draft of shadow weave for this profile. The full draft using the Powell method of drafting created from this profile is shown on page 92. The block designations have been added to illustrate how the profile applies. As discussed previously, we are designating the horizontal hatching areas as the pattern, and the vertical hatching as the background. We can see where the "A" block in the threading intersects with the "A" block in the treadling. Where this intersection occurs, we have

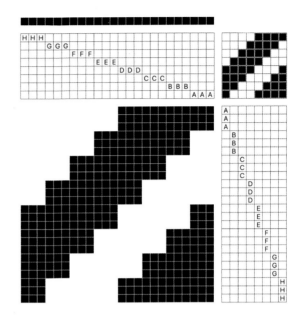

Combined eight-block profile draft

an area of pattern in the drawdown. This development of pattern area continues as the next blocks intersect in succession. These pattern blocks are labeled with their names in the drawdown.

All eight of the eight-shaft units have been added to the draft, each repeated three times. They are named above and beside where they appear in the threading and the treadling. We have also added in the standard Powell tie-up for this full threading and treadling draft. This draft is unidirectional and therefore is a unit weave draft.

We can also develop similar drafts for six shafts and four shafts. These are shown on page 93 with their respective profile drafts. In these drafts, three repeats of each block unit follow in order, as we did in the eight-shaft draft, starting from block "A." The blocks in the six-shaft draft are A, B, C, D, E, and F. The blocks in the four-shaft draft are A, B, C, and D. Refer back to the "Powell method units" graphic for a review of the units.

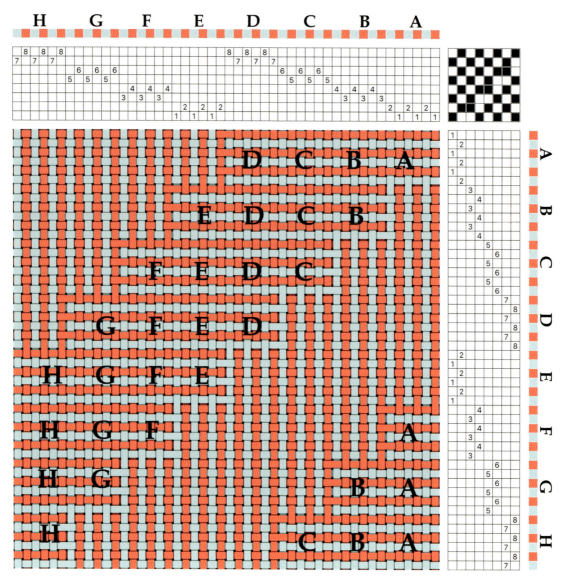

Eight-shaft Powell method draft with unit and block designations

In all three of these drafts developed from the combined profile drafts, half of the blocks create horizontal hatching and the other half vertical hatching. This is because the weave is based on a balanced twill in which half of the shafts are raised and the other half remain lowered. In the four-shaft draft, two blocks weave opposite the other two blocks. In the six-shaft draft it is 3 opposite 3, and in the eight-shaft draft it is 4 opposite 4. Powell lists the blocks that weave together on page 10 of her book and calls them "Sympathetic Joining of Units and/or Blocks" (1976). On the facing page is a graphic similar to Powell's. We can compare the eight-shaft list here with the eight-shaft draft labeled with block names above.

CHAPTER 6 Block Theory and Shadow Weave

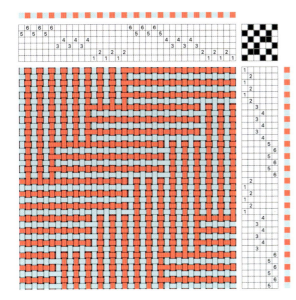

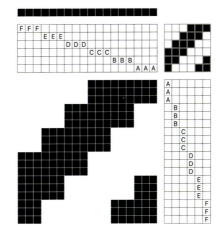

Six-shaft Powell method draft created using units A, B, C, D, E, and F from the profile draft

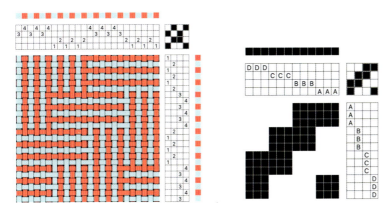

Four-shaft draft created using units A, B, C, and D from the profile draft

Design Blocks Weave Together			
	4 shafts	**6 shafts**	**8 shafts**
Block A weaves	A B	A B C	A B C D
Block B weaves	B C	B C D	B C D E
Block C weaves	C D	C D E	C D E F
Block D weaves	D A	D E F	D E F G
Block E weaves	– –	E F A	E F G H
Block F weaves	– –	F A B	F G H A
Block G weaves	– –	– –	G H A B
Block H weaves	– –	– –	H A B C

93

The Enigma of Shadow Weave Illuminated

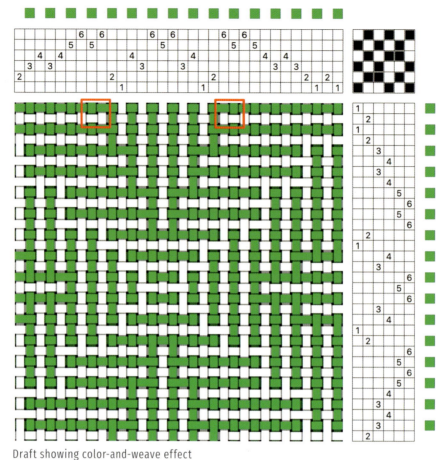

Draft showing color-and-weave effect

Block Theory and Designing Unique Drafts

This block theory framework gives you a place to start and to learn. Weavers can and do take this theory much further when designing their own drafts. We may say unit A is dark on 1 and light on 2, and my hope is that this will illuminate some of the enigmatic elements for you.

You might designate the units as something of your own choosing. You may say A is yellow green on 1 and magenta on 2. As long as you have some consistency and some kind of contrast within your project, shadow weave will ensue.

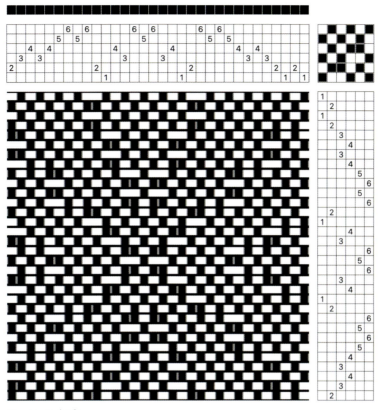

Structure draft

The Order of the Colors within the Units

Let's go back to our six-shaft point twill fashion draft and look again at the units used. If we wrote the units in sentence form for the sequential twill line as Powell did, the unit block C would be given as **5** 6 and also 6 **5**. Note it is **5** 6 when the twill line is ascending, and 6 **5** when the twill line is descending. In both designations we have dark on 5 and light on 6.

Then look at the area in the draft drawdown outlined by the red squares, where interlacements for those units are shown. The visual patterning within both of the boxes consists of a dark horizontal hatching above a white horizontal hatching. We conclude from this illustration that the **order** of the colors or values within the unit does not have a bearing on the visual effect. And we conclude further that it is the colorway that designates the block. The C block, in this case, always has dark on 5. This is what Atwater meant by the dark being "dominant." The dark threads define which unit we have. Other historical writers refer to this as the controlling end. If we look at the other units, we notice the color order is also opposite when ascending than it is when descending.

In the draft without the colorway there is no indication as to where the blocks are differentiated from one another. Here we have an example of how color-and-weave works, which is the creation of a visual patterning effect requiring **both** the structure and the colorway, and the effect is seemingly unrelated to either the weave structure or the use of color when considered individually. Such a statement brings forth the concept of the enigma, or at least, perhaps, a paradox. Two seemingly opposite, or at least very differing, things exist at the same time and create something new. This is one of the reasons shadow weave is so fascinating to me.

The Rules for Shadow Weave within Block Theory

Within block theory, each unit or nonunit structure is defined by applying certain rules. When the rules are followed, they will give us our woven cloth. The following are the rules for shadow weave:

1. The number of blocks available equals the number of shafts used.

2. Each block unit consists of two ends or picks—one dark and one light.

3. The colorway must be considered in the constellation of block units in addition to the shaft numbers, because it is a color-and-weave cloth. We remember color-and-weave is created by combining the weave structure **and** the colorway.

4. Block units may be used singly or they may be repeated at will in a draft to create wider or longer designs in the cloth.

5. Units may be threaded in any order.

6. In point twill fashion shadow weave, when our goal is to create symmetrical designs, some of the threads at the turning points are shared by two units. This means there will be an odd number of ends making up these reversals in the draft.

7. In order to maintain the odd number of threads at the reversals in symmetrical drafts, adjustments need to be made by either adding or deleting one thread in one unit.

8. Blocks will weave together at the same time. Because the weave is based on a balanced twill, half of the blocks will create horizontal hatching, the pattern area, and the other half will create vertical hatching, the background.

9. Each block unit is controlled or designated by a different shaft, which is sometimes called dominant. In most historical references the shaft carrying the dark is defined as controlling or dominant. This means, for example, that the block with dark on shaft 1 will be block A. This indicates again that the colorway is crucial for how the blocks function.

10. The color order within a unit changes when developing point twill fashion shadow weave. It is opposite when ascending than it is when descending.

The Trouble with Shadow Weave as a Block Weave—Ahh! The Enigma

There are also conflicting parameters, which show the problematic nature of shadow weave within block theory. They are also listed to illustrate the work required to illuminate shadow weave.

11. One type of draft, the unidirectional draft, is a pure unit weave.

12. Another type of draft, the draft with reversals in the threading or treadling, is a nonunit weave.

13. There are exceptions or adjustments required to create symmetrical drafts that contain reversals. Incidentals may be added to manage the adjustments needed.

14. Ends or picks may just as easily be deleted to manage the adjustments needed to create symmetrical drafts.

15. Asymmetrical drafts are just as wonderful and are valid cloth. No adjustments are made or needed at the reversals within these drafts.

16. Only Powell worked with shadow weave within block theory. Historically, other authors focused on the Atwater method, and they approached the weave based on twills.

17. Powell discusses block theory only briefly. She offers lists, which require considerable thought and interpretation, because today, perhaps, we do not have the same assumptions and knowledge of the theory of weaving with which she and other weavers of her day were familiar.

18. Drafts may be designed from profiles, with adjustments for some of the desired designs.

19. Drafts may also be designed based on twills, with adjustments for some of the desired designs.

20. Shadow weave has no distinctly separate or contrasting areas of background and of pattern, unless we designate the areas of hatching as such.

21. If we take into consideration the fact that shadow weave is the reverse on the reverse of the cloth, what happens to pattern and ground there?

22. A complicating factor when having a discussion about block weaves is that weavers tend to use the words "unit" and "block" interchangeably, as if they are the same.

Ultimately, we must conclude that shadow weave does not fit neatly or purely into block theory, especially when we are working with point twill fashion drafts. We can make comparisons to other structures that do flow easily with profiles, units, or blocks. However, these comparisons must be set aside and abandoned, since shadow weave functions as an entity unto itself. It must be managed in a manner specific to shadow weave.

CHAPTER 7

Designing Shadow Weave

Now that you know the basics, what would you like to design next in shadow weave? This chapter covers a few other concepts to expand your designing repertoire.

Extending Shadow Weave

In chapter 3, when discussing regular extended twill, it was mentioned that extending shadow weave was just a little trickier. However tricky it may be, we find that the trick involves understanding a simple concept—we must include the second set of units for creating longer twill fashion lines. The straight-twill fashion draft demonstrates this concept. Both the threading and the treadling begin with the units **1**-2, **3**-4, **5**-6, followed by the second set of units, **2**-1, **4**-3, **6**-5. We have used units A through F for six-shaft shadow weave when we follow this plan. The six units are then repeated to extend the featherstitching lines farther.

The next draft demonstrates how to create extended-point-twill fashion shadow weave. On either end of the threading and treadling we see a similar configuration as in the previous straight-twill fashion draft. This creates the longer diagonal lines in the patterning of the drawdown.

In the center of the threading we see point twill fashion threadings, and since this is as drawn in, we see the same in the treadling. Also, because this is a symmetrical draft, the points have been adjusted by removing one end in one of the units. The twill lines are slanted in either direction, depending on the wishes of the designer. Again, we use all of the units as we did in the straight-twill fashion draft. The slant of the point is repeated with the second set of units. The patterning lines of the point visible in the drawdown are deeper where the threading and treadling points are extended. We also see echoing featherstitching and hatching lines around the central motif, much like ripples on water. The design capabilities of this simple concept are enormous.

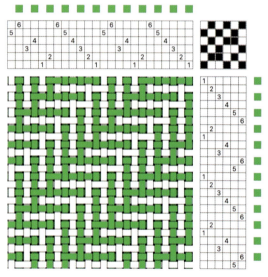

Extended-straight-twill fashion shadow weave draft

CHAPTER 7 Designing Shadow Weave

Extended-point-twill fashion shadow weave draft

The conclusion for switch drafts is that the structure remains, but the color-and-weave effect is altered significantly by switching **one** of the colorways. We can create this effect by switching either the threading or the treadling colorway. If we switch both the threading and the treadling colorways, we are back to a regular shadow weave draft with the featherstitching distinctly made with a single color or value.

It is also important to note that we are able to see straight-lined geometrics in these graphics on paper or in our computers. However, in the actual cloth the lines are softened, and the switch draft lines approximate a visual effect more closely related to the regular shadow weave draft. Switch draft is an excellent design option to consider, especially if you are wanting softer lines in your project.

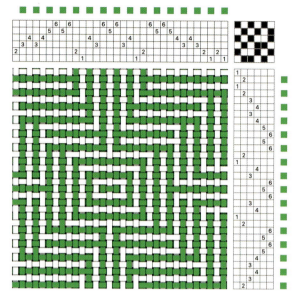

One repeat of the inverted switch draft

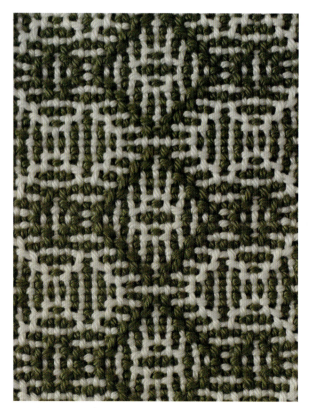

Regular symmetrical shadow weave

Switch draft cloth

CHAPTER 7 Designing Shadow Weave

Designing with Profile Drafts

For this design exercise we are following in the footsteps of Marian Powell by designing shadow weave drafts from a profile draft. There are many profile drafts in references online or in print. Look for your favorites.

Another option is designing your own profile drafts. The main thing to remember is there are as many design blocks as there are shafts. Here is an example of a combined profile draft with eight design blocks.

This profile draft translates into an eight-shaft full shadow weave draft. Refer to the Powell method units to see how the draft was obtained. Because this draft has reversals, there have been some adjustments made there. You may also note this profile draft is not as drawn in, perhaps following in the footsteps of Mary Meigs Atwater.

The sky's the limit when creating shadow weave from profile drafts. Do you like organic designs? Or are geometrics more appealing? Perhaps you would like to create asymmetrical symmetrical shadow weave drafts.

Profile draft with eight design blocks #1

The Enigma of Shadow Weave Illuminated

Full draft developed from profile draft #1

CHAPTER 7 Designing Shadow Weave

Options for Changing and Working with Units

Another drafting-design method is to vary how we move from one unit to another in our drafts. We have seen previously in the regular shadow weave drafts that we change units merely by adding them in sequence or in sections of repeated units. For these drafts we are keeping one dark and one light alternating throughout the entire draft. Another method is to repeat the value or color in the threading or the treadling, by placing two of the same exact value of threads side by side. Remember if we have a unit with dark as one of the threads of the unit and light as the second, we must also have the opposite to obtain our full complement of combinations. In the next draft we can see the shifting configuration of the units.

Where the double dark threads are located, we have an A unit adjacent to a D unit.

We still have some resemblance of the basic four diamonds. However, we have shifted the colorway of the featherstitching and the direction of the hatching, which gives a visual effect similar to broken twill. We will also have more-distinct dark lines where the two darks run through the cloth. This drafting method would work equally well by drafting two lights together. We could also draft any two colors together if we are using contrast of hue. Incidentally, the cloth from this draft is essentially the same on the reverse.

Changing units in the draft—double dark threads

107

One other way to change units is to repeat the ends on the same shaft or treadle, as shown in the next draft. Here we have repeated the threads on shaft 2; one is dark and one is light. These threads will be threaded into separate heddles. This again has a configuration with an A unit adjacent to a D unit. We can change units in this manner by using any of the units. The colorway alternates dark and light throughout this draft. We also have two threads, a dark and a light, floating together inside a channel of two-thread floats occurring along the length of the cloth. This structure does not detract from the validity of our cloth. The starting place for designing this draft was the same six-shaft point twill fashion draft used as a starting place for the switch draft, shown on page 102. We have only altered the threading. The treadling remains the same. In this new draft the central motif of the four diamonds has changed significantly.

Then, what if we make this draft as drawn in? Only vestiges of our central diamonds remain. And here we have a new design, geometric and interesting.

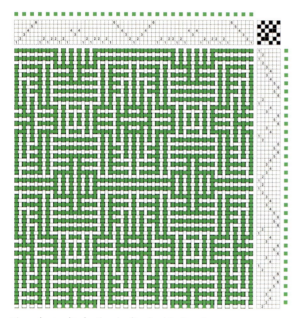

Changing units in the draft—doubled ends

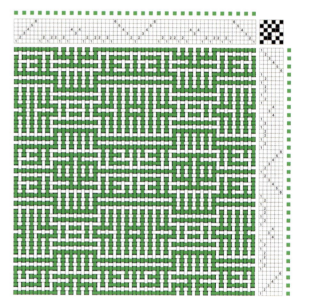

Changing units in the draft—doubled ends, as drawn in

CHAPTER 7 Designing Shadow Weave

Full draft developed from profile draft #2

Eight-block profile draft #2

What if we change the sequencing of the units? Profile draft #2 is an eight-block profile draft, which is translated into the eight-shaft shadow weave full draft.

There are several things to notice in this draft. The second set of units, which are defined as dark on the evens and light on odds in chapter 6, now appears as a straight-twill fashion line in the threading and the treadling. In the previous drafts used as illustrations, these units appear as the offset-twill fashion line. Conversely, in this draft the units defined as dark on the odds and light on evens now create the offset-twill fashion line.

109

As a result the hatching occurs in the opposite direction, and the featherstitching is in the opposite color.

You will also notice there is a single thread at the end of the threading and the treadling. This is merely the result of the designer's preference to begin each draft with a dark thread. There is a reversal or point at the edges of the repeat of this draft, and in order to make this a symmetrical shadow weave draft, an adjustment needs to be made. An incidental light thread has been added at the end of the draft for this purpose. Looking back to the profile draft, we also see that the reversal has been managed by ending the profile repeat with block C, instead of progressing up to block D. We also notice that the blocks in the profile draft do not fall in consecutive order. This means the blocks or units may be in any order.

Another possibility of manipulating the blocks is to create a broken-twill fashion effect, as shown in profile draft #3. This is done by skipping four steps around the eight-shaft twill circle. We make the skip around the twill circle when we go from block E to block H, and when we go from block A to block E. We see the distinct lines in the profile draft.

The full draft created from the profile creates the broken-twill fashion effect in two ways. One is by repeating the sequence of units H, G, F, and E twice. The other is by placing units A and E adjacent to each other at the lower reversals in the middle of the draft, which creates the sequence of double dark threads. Interestingly, we have not made adjustments to these two reversals, and it still creates a symmetrical shadow weave draft.

Eight-block profile draft #3

CHAPTER 7 Designing Shadow Weave

Full draft developed from profile draft #3

How many "rules" did we break to create this draft? And yet, it is an appealing symmetrical shadow weave draft.

Let's take this draft one step further by repeating it two times in both the threading and the treadling. This creates a central square motif with an eight-pointed star in the middle. Always remember to look at the additional repeat to see the motifs forming at the edges of your single repeat.

The Enigma of Shadow Weave Illuminated

Two repeats of the full draft developed from a profile draft #3

"Rules"

When approaching any new subject or process, it is always good to learn the "rules." There are always basic parameters. I think about my career of teaching medical processes. It is important to know the basics, however, since as you encounter different patients or different situations, you have to *apply* the basics. In medical settings we use critical thinking to apply them. Once in a while the basics are really bent and stretched to meet the needs of a patient.

Weaving is no different. We can push and pull the basics when we are designing to create fabulous new and interesting cloth. Weavers will always discuss the merits of the new design, and whether it still falls within a given category or structure. Perhaps this is what makes it art.

Multiple-Shaft Shadow Weave

Following the parameters outlined in this book, there is minimal advantage of increasing the shafts to increase the design capabilities. That is because we merely make the featherstitching lines longer and increase the plain weave hatching areas between the featherstitching. Compare the six-shaft draft, at the right, to a similar draft on twelve shafts, shown on page 114.

Of course, there may be reasons to weave the twelve-shaft cloth. One reason is to increase the scale of the project. Envision a large art piece mounted high on a wall, which would be viewed from below. Larger areas of hatching for this purpose may be more desirable to the designer.

Also remember the multiple-shaft design capabilities presented by Elizabeth Lang and Erica Voolich in their book *Parallel Shadow Weave*, for more than eight shafts. For those interested in multiple-shaft designing, it's very useful to pursue their method for further study.

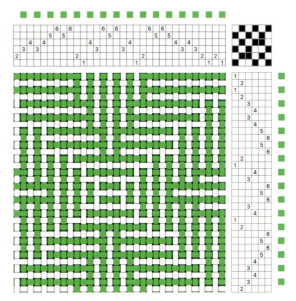

Six-shaft point-twill fashion draft

The Enigma of Shadow Weave Illuminated

Twelve-shaft point-twill fashion draft

Does Shadow Weave Make Lace?

During the course of researching shadow weave, I wove a cloth to demonstrate the structure of the weave. The colorway was eliminated in the design, and the cloth was woven with the same exact color of yarn for both the entire warp and the entire weft. The cloth was held up to view at arm's length. As serendipity would have it, there happened to be a window behind the cloth. Oh, goodness, it looked like lace, and the structure patterning viewed in the cloth was seen as shadow and light. Test this out for yourself, since this effect can be viewed also in cloth with dark and light threads. Creating cloth using only one yarn and a shadow weave draft is another design option. It would be especially effective when considering the shadow weave structure for window treatments.

CHAPTER 7 Designing Shadow Weave

Shadow weave cloth woven with one weft

Shadow weave cloth woven with one weft, backlight

115

Using Other Types of Design Contrast

We have discussed the contrast of value in shadow weave, and it is still the best choice to show off your efforts to weave this end-by-end and pick-by-pick colorway. There are several other types of contrast to consider, however, including the contrasts of hue, color intensity, scale, and texture. We may wish to use these additional contrasts judiciously, because shadow weave has a lot going on with just value contrast. Why would you make the effort to weave shadow weave if you did not maintain the design to some extent?

Adding different colors in the warp or weft also represents endless possibilities. Weavers love to play with color, and shadow weave offers a huge array of color choices, including using varying degrees of contrast of value, contrast of hue, or contrast of color intensity. Our knowledge of color theory will aid us as we explore. Ultimately, however, when playing with colors, it comes down to what colors or color combinations the weaver prefers.

Remember that the highest contrast of hues is any two colors across from one another on the color wheel. An example is red and green. Contrast of color intensity begins with a relatively pure color and contrasts it with a tint, shade, or tone of that color or another color. An example is light grayed green and green.

One place to begin your color exploration is to change just one yarn in the weft, as shown at right. The resulting cloth would have three colors. Perhaps we like the light and decide to use it in both the warp and the weft. Then change the dark weft to an analogous hue. By making this one simple change, we add interest in our cloth. Many viewers will take a second look to see what is really going on in the cloth.

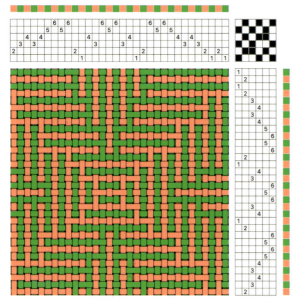
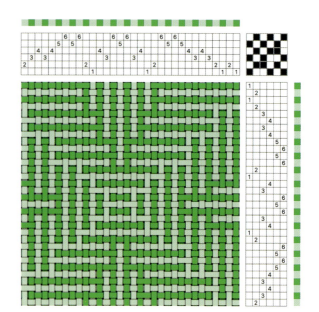

Six-shaft point-twill fashion drafts in other colorways

CHAPTER 7 Designing Shadow Weave

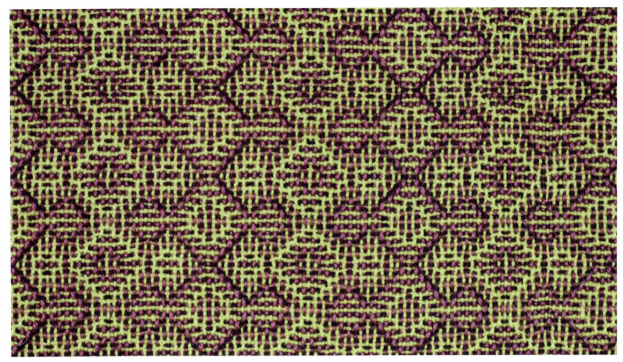

Shadow weave cloth woven with three colors

What if we warped with two colors and used two completely different colors in the weft? This gives us a cloth with four colors. Having some knowledge about color mixing will serve for this exercise. The color gamp towels were designed and woven using four colors in this way.

Lunatic Fringe Yarns color gamp towel sample

117

Another example shows how amazing this kind of color mixing can be. This warp is a very calm purple and green. When mixed with red and gold, a vibrant and interesting cloth is the result.

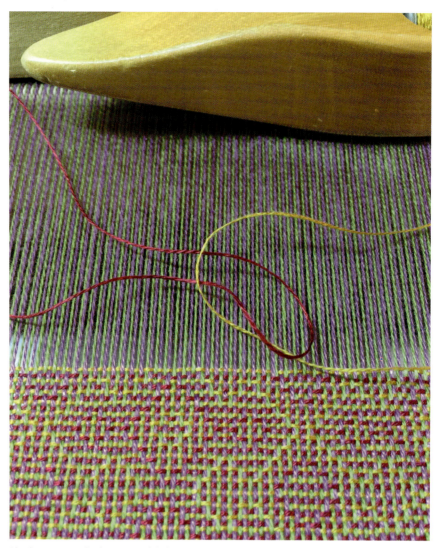

Shadow weave cloth woven with four colors, on loom and after finishing

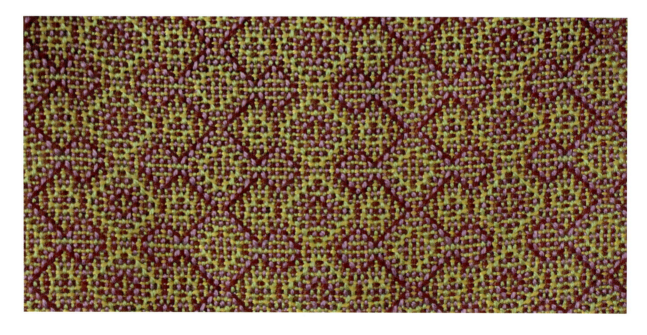

CHAPTER 7 Designing Shadow Weave

What if we vary the colors by creating stripes in either warp or weft to accentuate certain motifs? Do a little computer weaving, otherwise known as using your weaving software, to try different colors in your draft. The next draft shows a variation in the colorway for the unique profile draft shown in the section of this chapter called "Designing with Profile Drafts." Start with two basic colors—magenta and very light pink. Then change a few dark threads in both the warp and the weft to dark teal. This accentuates the small diamonds in the center.

Then change a few light ends in the center of the warp to yellow. Note we are keeping the value contrast similar for our new threads.

When we draft two repeats in both the warp and weft, we discover that the elongated diamonds are accentuated by the yellow, and there is a greenish cast when it mixes with the teal. Also, other interesting motifs appear at the edges of the design repeats. This has been said before, and it bears repeating. The surprising discoveries there at the edges are also limitless.

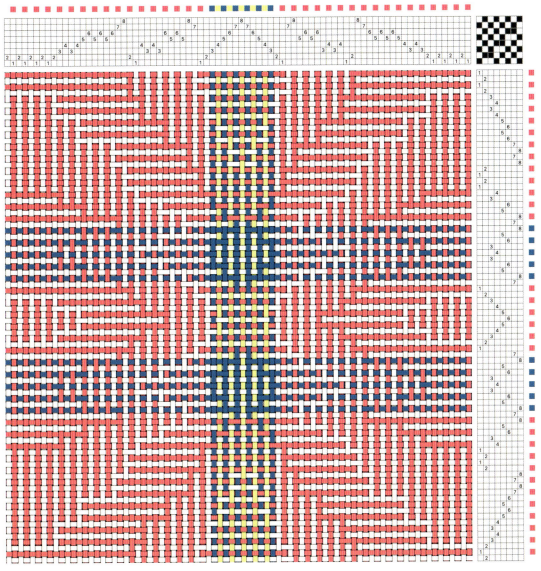

Full draft developed from profile draft #1 with stripes

119

The Enigma of Shadow Weave Illuminated

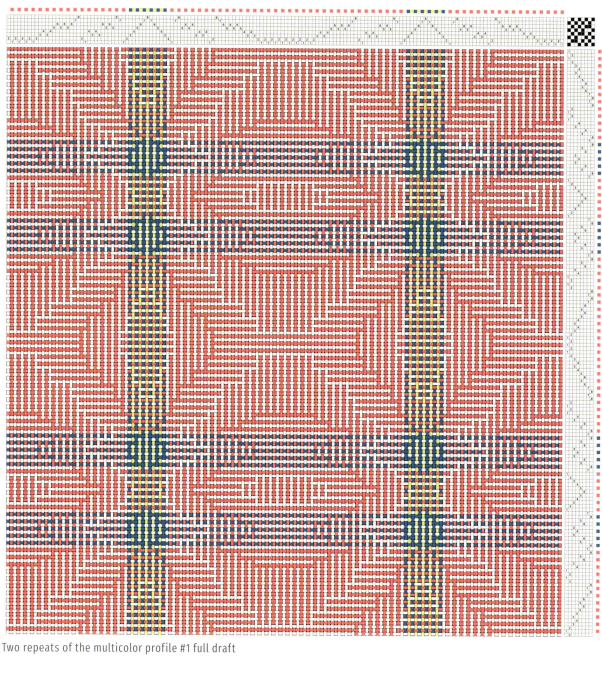

Two repeats of the multicolor profile #1 full draft

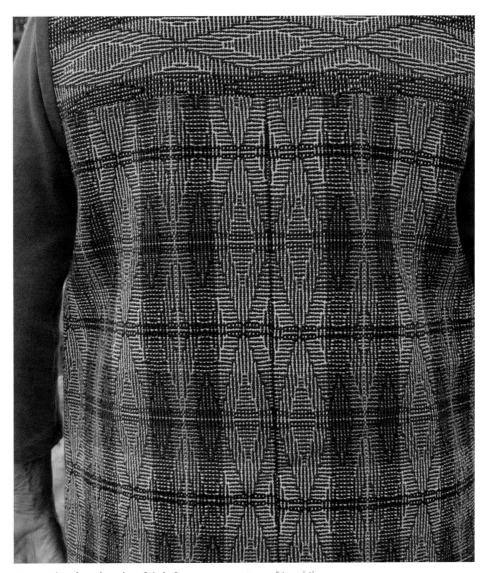

Warp and weft stripes in a fabric for a vest, courtesy of Jenni Jimmerson

Three sets of light/dark 5/2 cotton yarns, plus an accent color, were used in this example of warp and weft stripes. The three are 5 Purple with avocado, forest green with safari, and birch with bark. The accent is teal. The resulting color effect is beautiful and surprising. There really are dark greens in this fabric.

Weavers frequently consider contrast of scale when planning projects. One example was mentioned when considering shadow weave woven on more than eight shafts. A large wall piece requires a bolder scale. A scarf in finer yarns requires a finer scale. This design concept is also subject to the weaver's preference.

Contrast of scale can also be applied to the various yarns chosen for a single project. What if we use thick and thin yarns in place of the two values of yarn? This opens another huge area for weaving shadow weave. We may wish to double or triple the yarns of one weft to emphasize that color in our project, while keeping the sett balanced. Or we may plan a warp of entirely one size of yarn and then use thick and thin yarns in the weft.

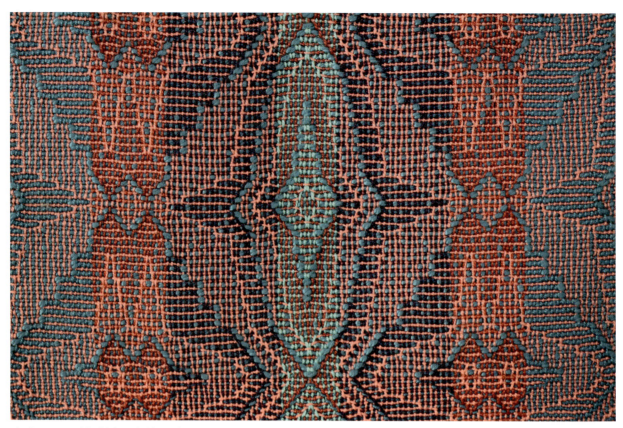

Cloth woven with thick and thin weft
The warp is 10/2 cotton sett at 24 epi. The weft is 10/2 cotton for the light & 3/2 cotton for the dark.

This plan will offer additional texture in the hand of the cloth. We may also note, since we are only changing something in the weft, that both balanced shadow weave and the thick and thin can be woven on this same warp. We could possibly use both types of cloth in the same garment for contrasting areas in the overall design. The warp for the example pictured is entirely 10/2 cotton. The weft is 10/2 cotton for the light and 3/2 cotton for the dark. Warp stripes are also used to accentuate certain motifs.

What if we change the sett of our shadow weave? This concept offers a wide range of options, from somewhat warp faced to completely warp faced. This cloth is made with 3/2 cotton sett at 16 ends per inch, which is a little close to obtain a balanced weave. The result is a cloth leaning toward warp faced. The light yarn in the warp is copper, and gold was used as light in the weft. Forest is the dark yarn throughout. The motifs are a little elongated, and this cloth makes beautiful and sturdy place mats for the table.

Moderately warp-faced shadow weave made with 3/2 cotton, courtesy of Greta Ankeny

CHAPTER 7 Designing Shadow Weave

Balanced cloth and rep weave woven on the same warp after changing the sett

What if we change the sett in addition to using thick and thin weft, and make our cloth completely weft faced? Then we are creating a rep weave. While rep weave is not covered in this book, it is important to share this piece of information—any shadow weave draft can be used for rep weave. For this we use thick and thin in the weft in place of the light and the dark picks on the draft. Many beautiful rep weave designs are possible, and you can weave a rep weave cloth and a balanced cloth on the same warp if you resley. Can you envision rep weave place mats and a balanced cloth for napkins or the tablecloth?

Contrast of texture is the final type to consider. It is a little more difficult to use in color-and-weave. However, it is still one of the contrast options. If we remember that the contrast of value is the most important for creating our visual effect, and we use it in combination with contrast of texture, we may be able to find viable options. It remains on a list of weaves for further study.

A final note of encouragement, or perhaps admonishment, comes from Marian Powell herself. She writes twice in a single paragraph in her book in capital letters to "PLEASE-PLEASE-PLEASE make samples." She followed her own advice. There are more than 1,000 samples representing as many drafts in her book alone, and I have seen many more additional samples using threadings from her book, which proves she continued her rigorous sampling practice. This is also proof to me that she was just as exacting and strict in her weaving practice as Atwater and Tidball. We weavers know sampling is important, and we get to decide how we wish to approach our own weaving process.

Okay, the teacher in me says, "Ready, set, go." These are only a few of the possibilities in shadow weave. Please continue your exploration to reveal more of the enigma. What designs will you create in shadow weave?

CHAPTER 8

Doubleweave?

There are two questions related to doubleweave to consider when studying and weaving shadow weave. Answers to these questions were found nowhere in an extensive literature review. Some conclusions are offered for your consideration. I invite and welcome further conversations relative to what is being proposed.

Is There Doubleweave in Shadow Weave?

Doubleweave is defined in a similar way by both Madelyn van der Hoogt and Doramay Keasbey. Keasbey's definition says, "Two or more warps and wefts make possible double cloth or multiple layers, each layer consisting of its own warp interlaced by its weft" (2005, page 195). Atwater gives a similar description: "Double weaving consists in making two separate fabrics, one above the other" (1928 and 1951, page 255).

Doubleweave can be woven from several different drafts, one of which is similar to the Powell shadow weave method, drafted sequentially. Another is similar to the Atwater shadow weave method drafted in a parallel format.

For both doubleweave and shadow weave, we struggle to demonstrate the full structure on paper or in electronic drafts. We could say this equally true of rep weave drafts. This is because these weaves are three-dimensional, and we are attempting to demonstrate them in a two-dimensional format. We must weave the cloth or examine it to identify its multidimensional characteristic.

Next take a look at two drafts. The first is Atwater's draft (e) from the *Shuttle-Craft Guild Bulletin*, February 1942, which has been converted to a Powell method draft. The second is a four-shaft, straight-twill-fashion, Powell shadow weave draft. As previously stated, Atwater called her draft "Double Weave." While comparing these two drafts in our limited two-dimensional format, we can see there are areas of the same structure in both drafts.

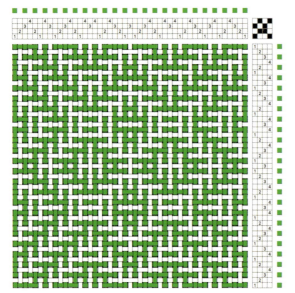

Powell conversion of draft (e) from February 1942; called "Double Weave" by Atwater

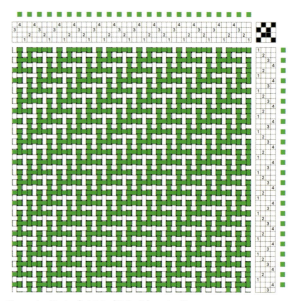

Four-shaft straight-twill fashion draft

Cloth woven from draft (e) from February 1942; called "Double Weave" by Atwater

Cloth woven from the four-shaft straight-twill fashion draft

If we select one line of diagonal two-thread floats, we know we have light featherstitching on one side and dark on the reverse of the cloth. The light line of featherstitching is made up of one weft and one warp. The dark featherstitching on the other side of the cloth is made up of another set of one weft and one warp. Each of these two layers consists of its own warp interlaced by its weft. We find these channels of doubleweave in all shadow weave where there are lines of two-thread floats.

This brings us to the next question. If Atwater called her cloth "Double Weave," would not the other also be doubleweave?

Tidball described shadow weave as a textural weave. While the plain weave is flat, the surrounding featherstitching rises a bit above the surface created by the plain weave. This is a function of the presence of the two layers.

The next point to make is hearsay, really. It boils down to a "he said / she said" exercise. And it is so very pertinent to this discussion. We have all had informal conversations at national conferences in which we learn tremendous lessons. There was a conversation about weaving topics at one such conference, and a statement about doubleweave was offered. The person making the statement knew and worked closely with Paul O'Connor, a well-known weaver and author on the topic of doubleweave. The person said that Mr. O'Connor said, "If you can put the head of a pin in it, it's doubleweave." What a revelation this is when we apply it to shadow weave.

To demonstrate this concept, look at the two photos on page 128. These are of two sides of the same shadow weave cloth. A knitting needle has been inserted into the diagonal featherstitching line. While this is not exactly the head of a pin, it does give you a distinctive demonstration. In the first picture the needle is inserted under the light featherstitching. Then the cloth was merely turned over and the needle was inserted into a similar channel on the reverse.

Needle under the light featherstitching

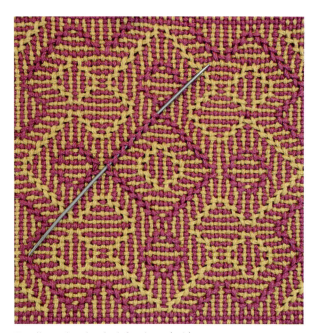
Needle under the dark featherstitching

Is this "true" doubleweave?—probably not. These layers, if taken alone, would likely not stand as valid cloth. On the other hand, we can see there are two very distinctive layers at the featherstitching. These layers are held together by the surrounding plain weave structure.

Tidball was correct in her statement that "the fabric can hardly be visualized with out seeing it" (*Shuttle Craft Guild Handweaver's Bulletin*, July 1953, page 8). This statement implies the difficulty of showing the full nature of the cloth in two dimensions or in descriptions. It also validates the enigmatic nature of shadow weave.

To expand this concept, the fabric can hardly be visualized without spending time at the loom weaving it. Powell certainly supports this notion with her recommendation to do sampling. I encourage you to weave some shadow weave cloth, so you can see the phenomenon occurring at the featherstitching for yourself.

From What Structure Did Atwater Derive Shadow Weave?

Multiple authors state that Atwater derived shadow weave from rep weave. Tidball was the first, when she said Atwater derived it "without a doubt" from rep weave. Did the authors who wrote after Tidball take this statement as true and then continue the fact?

Let's review Atwater's first article, when she presented shadow weave to the weaving world. She gave three drafts for her new "shadow" weave. Then next she included two additional drafts called "Double Weave." Both drafts are made with parallel threadings, which is one of the types of drafts used for doubleweave.

If we sift back through the *Shuttle-Craft Guild Bulletin* by Atwater around the time of her publication about shadow weave, we find what she published about rep weave. There are three significant issues containing rep weave information—July 1940, August 1942, and March 1947. All three issues contain similar information and drafts for weaving upholstery fabric.

Since the August 1942 issue was published closest to the time of Atwater's first article about shadow weave, let's look at the three rep weave threadings given there.

4		4		4		4		
	3		3		3		3	
						2		2		2		2
							1		1		1		1

Threading (a), called "Swedish Rep"

				4	4	4	4								
3	3	3	3					3	3	3	3				
												2	2	2	2
1	1	1	1	1	1	1	1	1	1	1	1	1	1	1	1

Threading (b), called "Bronson Rep"

8		8		8										
	7		7		7									
					6		6		6					
						5		5		5				
											4		4		4
												3		3		3
														2		2		2
															1		1		1

Threading (c), called "Two-Way Rep"
The *Shuttle-Craft Guild Bulletin*, August 1942, page 3

These threadings do not contain the parallel threadings Atwater used for presenting shadow weave. They also are not similar to the threadings used for the "Double Weave" drafts offered by her in February 1942.

Additionally, it is important to note the kind of rep weave that Atwater proposed is not what we think of as rep weave today. In a few places she refers to it as "Peruvian rep weave." In the *Shuttle-Craft Guild Bulletin* of July 1940, she discussed using 5/2 cotton for both the warp and the weft. There is no mention of thick and thin weft. She does recommend to sett the warp closely at 40 ends per inch. The recommended weft for the (a) and (b) drafts in the August 1942 issue is "course" weft. Again there is no mention of using both thick and thin weft. If the course weft is used, cloth from these descriptions would be a warp-faced cloth with even ribs.

We could conclude, then, from these details that it is just as likely Atwater derived shadow weave from doubleweave as it is that she derived it from rep weave. Mary Black said in *The Key to Weaving* that many of the early Atwater samples and notes had been destroyed (1980, page 302). So the definitive answer to this question will likely remain an enigma, unless other historical documents can be found. Ultimately, the main conclusion to gain from this discussion is that shadow weave, doubleweave, and rep weave are cousins, or perhaps sisters. As we study further and weave more, the similarities are discovered.

CHAPTER 9

Shadow Weave Projects

◇◇◇

We weavers love to share our experiences with projects in study groups, and I would like to share information about these projects in the spirit of a guild group. For connecting with other weavers, I encourage you to find a guild near you. Plus, there are many online options for connecting with other fiber enthusiasts.

Shadow weave scarves
From left:
10/2 cotton scarf in light rust and 10 Blue Green, courtesy of Julie Gerrard
20/2 cotton scarf in Teal and other colors, courtesy of Cynthia Newman
8/2 Tencel Scarf in straw and Pompeii, courtesy of Vila Cox

Projects: Three Scarves and Three Towels

Included in the project descriptions are tips and suggestions for managing each weave. To take best advantage of the tips, I encourage you to read through all of the projects before embarking on your journey with a single project. Know that I tend to use a laissez-faire approach to weaving. My favorite grandmother frequently advised, "Just enough, but not too much." Her philosophy was usually applied to cooking when she gave it, but I like to apply it to weaving as well. Basically, if it works for you, go for it. If not, don't.

Shadow weave towels

Coral Challenge Scarf
Project Weaving Record & Notes

Draft:
Marian Powell Draft # 6-16-9 (1976, page 177)

Warp & Weft Yarn:
5/2 pearl cotton, 2,100 yards per pound

Warp Colors:
Lunatic Fringe Yarns 5 Purple and Coral

Weft Colors:
Lunatic Fringe Yarns 5 Purple and Copper

Sett: 15 epi

Denting:
1 per dent in a 15-dent reed

Total Ends: 138

Total Picks: 1,232, calculated by multiplying the number of picks in one repeat by the number of repeats woven

Weaving Width in Reed: 9.2 inches

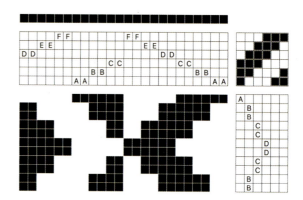

Coral scarf profile draft

Weaver's Note:
This scarf won first place in the Lunatic Fringe Yarns Coral Challenge, held in 2018.

Coral Challenge Scarf

The Enigma of Shadow Weave Illuminated

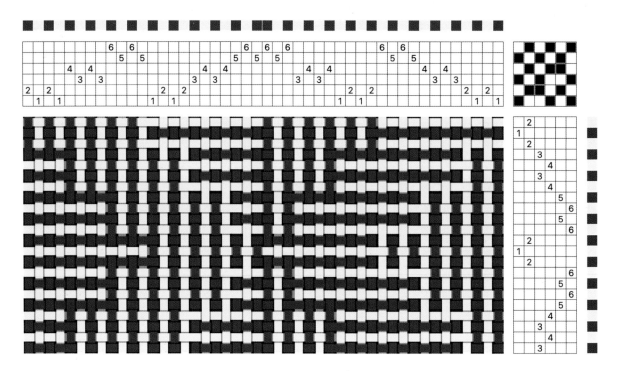

Full draft for the Coral Challenge Scarf

Warp Winding:

Wind a warp 3.5 yards long. This provides you with 83 inches for the body of your scarf, 9 inches at the beginning of your weaving for fringe, and a generous loom waste of about 36 inches. The ending fringe can be part of your ending loom waste. There is also an opportunity to weave a short sample to add to your documentation. Dress your loom, using your favorite method.

The threading for this warp is three repeats of the draft. Note the threading has dark ends at the beginning and at the end of one repeat. There are also double darks in the middle of the one repeat. There are sixty-six light ends and seventy-two dark ends. I prefer to wind one dark thread and one light thread together as one at the warping board. The two are held with a finger between them in two places—as they come off the cones and as they are wound onto the warping board. Then for this warp, I added the six extra dark ends at the end of my winding.

When I am warping, those few extra dark ends get popped into place across the warp. I warp front to back, so this designing step happens in the reed. It involves counting dents to figure out where those extra dark ends go. With a little care and focus, they are placed right where they are needed.

I can hear the next question—the extra dark ends are now out of place from the cross, and don't they get tangled? Here is my answer. I use what some have called the "yank and crank" method of warping, although what I really do is more like "smooth and crank." Once the warp is completely threaded and tied to the back beam bar, I go to the front and begin the smoothing with my hands. There is no tensioning method used at this point, other than this smoothing. The additional tension placed on the warp as it passes through the reed and the heddles completes the job. The 5/2 cotton yarn is forgiving and lends itself to this process.

Weaving Notes:

Leave about 9 inches of warp for the fringe at the beginning of your scarf.

Insert about four or five picks of contrasting-color waste weft yarn at the beginning of your scarf. This will stay in place until you twist your fringe.

Begin your weaving with five picks of 5 Purple on treadles 1-2-1-2-1. I like this method of beginning with the dark yarn because it gives a foundation or a framing hem for the end of your scarf.

Then begin the first treadling repeat with Copper on treadle 2.

Repeat the treadling fifty-six times, for a length of about 82 or 83 inches. I have to say, I am not very exacting when it comes to these measurements. To me enough is enough. This approach applies to picks per inch (ppi) as well, and at this point in my weaving career, I do not count or measure ppi. If the sett is correct and there is a nice beat, you will obtain a balanced cloth.

Repeat the five picks of 5 Purple to provide the same framing hem at this end of your scarf.

Insert more waste yarn and leave another 9 inches for the second fringe.

Weave your documentation sample, if there is enough warp remaining, and remove your fabulous scarf from the loom.

Finishing Method:

Complete the twisting of the fringe. I cut the waste yarn back bit by bit as I complete the twisting. I also twist the fringe without hemstitching. I add a lot of twist—as much as the yarn will allow, which holds the weft very well in place. This is my preferred method. If you prefer another, please feel free to finish the scarf as you wish.

Wet-finish your scarf. Remember that shadow weave needs this step to allow the featherstitching to relax into place. This scarf was wet-finished and dried in the washing machine and dryer after fringe twisting. Trim the raw ends of the fringe knots to provide a pleasing finish.

Press your scarf lightly with an iron, following recommendations for your fiber type.

The finished scarf length is 70 inches, plus 12 total inches of fringe. The finished width is 7.75 inches.

Fringe-twisting method

Gray & Brown Cotton Scarf
Project Weaving Record & Notes

Draft: Original, Profile 1

Warp Yarn: 10/2 pearl cotton, 4,200 yards per pound

Warp Color: Lunatic Fringe Yarns Light Gray & Copper

Weft Yarn & Color: Same as the warp

Sett: 24 epi

Denting: 2 per dent in a 12-dent reed

Total Ends: 235

Total Picks: Weave a scarf to your desired length. Adjust this length according to your own sampling, experience, and project design.

This scarf was woven to a length of about 75 inches. This woven length will account for about 20% take-up and shrinkage.

Weaving Width in Reed: 9.8 inches

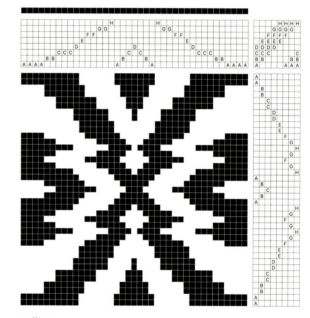

Profile 1

Gray & Brown Cotton Scarf

Warp Winding:

I will leave the warp length to be wound to your own calculations and discretion.

Repeat the threading three times and add one dark end on one to frame your scarf in darks on both selvages. Follow the suggestions for winding in the Coral Challenge Project. Dress your loom by using your favorite method.

Weaving Notes:

The treadling for this draft is not the same as the threading.

I had some fun playing with various treadlings for this scarf. You have learned how to design in shadow weave from reading the previous chapters, so ready, set, go. A couple of suggestions for alternate treadlings are to weave as drawn in, weave a regular point twill treadling from 1 through 8 and back, or weave through the eight shadow weave Powell method units in straight-twill fashion or point twill fashion. Of course you will be weaving these using a light/dark sequencing throughout with two shuttles.

Finishing Method:

This scarf was wet-finished and dried by machine first, then hemmed.

The hem is rolled to a scant quarter of an inch. This may be stitched by hand or on the machine. I stitched the hem on the machine with a coordinating color of thread.

Finished length is 64 inches. Finished width is 8.5 inches.

Gray & Brown Scarf, details of the treadlings

CHAPTER 9 Shadow Weave Projects

One repeat of the draft for the Gray & Brown Scarf

8/2 Tencel Scarf
Project Weaving Record & Notes

Draft: Original, Profile 12

Warp Yarn: 8/2 Tencel®, 3,360 yards per pound

Warp Color: WEBS Straw and Pompeii

Weft Yarn & Color: Same as the warp

Sett: 20 epi

Denting: 2 per dent in a 10-dent reed

Total Ends: 219

Total Picks: The scarf was woven to a length of about 75 inches. Adjust this length according to your own sampling and experience.

Weaving Width in Reed: 10.95 inches

Profile 12

8/2 Tencel Scarf, courtesy of Vila Cox

Warp Winding:

I will leave the warp length to be wound to your own calculations and discretion.

The full threading is given. Dress your loom, using your favorite method. Warp section A, then section B, and finally section C. Read these sections from the right, and refer to the full draft for clarification.

My friend Vila Cox of Warped & Wonderful wove this scarf. She started with my Profile 12 and did a bit of designing from there to make pleasing scarf motifs. For a design challenge, determine what she changed in her full draft, compared to the profile draft.

Weaving Notes:

The treadling is not the same as the threading. However, the treadling does follow the profile exactly. Weave section A, starting from the top. Then weave section B from the top to complete one repeat of the treadling. You will be weaving using a light/dark sequencing throughout with two shuttles.

Finishing Method:

This scarf was wet-finished and dried by machine. Twisted fringe was added.

Finished length is 66 inches, plus fringe. Finished width is 9.5 inches.

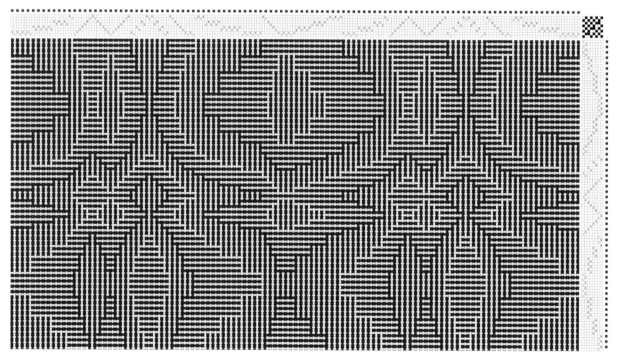

Vila's design for the full draft used for the 8/2 Tencel Scarf

CHAPTER 9 Shadow Weave Projects

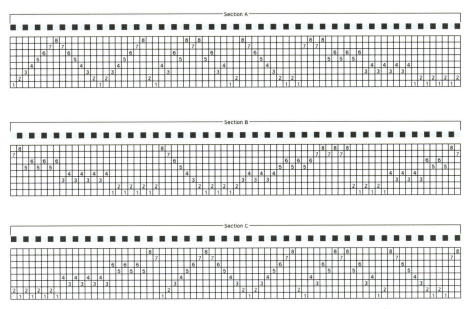

Threading for the 8/2 Tencel Scarf

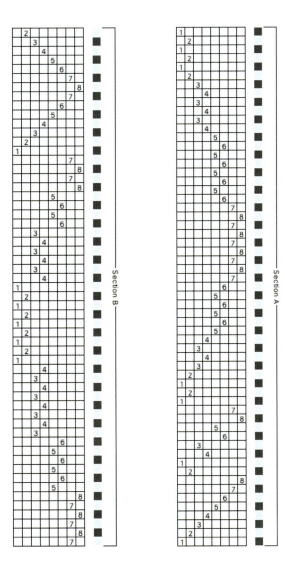

Treadling for the 8/2 Tencel Scarf
For one repeat of the treadling, start weaving from the top of section A and then continue from the top of section B for the remainder of the repeat.

Kitchen Towel

Project Weaving Record & Notes

Draft: Marian Powell Threading Draft # 8-8-12 (1976, page 213)

Warp Yarn: 5/2 pearl cotton, 2,100 yards per pound

Warp Color: UKI Bermuda Blue and Crab

Weft Yarn & Color: Same as the warp

Sett: 15 epi

Denting: 1 per dent in a 15-dent reed

Total Ends: 257

Total Picks: Adjust length to be woven to your own calculations and discretion.

For towels, a pleasing ratio between the width and the length is the golden ratio, which is about 1.6. For example, if I have a weaving width of 15 inches, I will multiply by 1.6 to obtain a length of 24 inches. This is the general rule of thumb I use. It is affected by the patterning created and the repeats in the draft for the cloth. I apply this rule to the on-loom dimensions. After wet finishing, an approximation of the ratio remains, even when considering shrinkage and take-up.

Weaving Width in Reed: 17.13 inches

Kitchen Towel

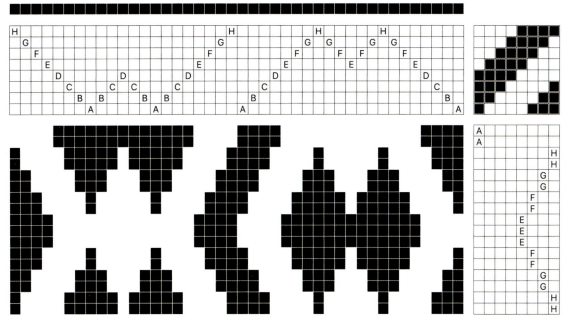

Profile draft

149

Warp Winding:

I will leave the warp length to be wound to your own calculations and discretion.

This threading was designed so one of the main motifs was centered. The threading consists of about two and a half repeats of the Powell draft. Straight-twill fashion threading of eight units was added on both sides of the towel to create some framing ripples. I encourage you to create your own final project weaving drafts in this manner. Powell boils her draft repeats down to the lowest possible denominator and gives us one repeat. In her era they understood there would be planning for a full project draft, with her drafts used as merely a starting place. Most of them require a portion of a repeat in addition to several repeats to obtain full width with a balanced or symmetrical design.

Follow the suggestions for winding your warp in the Coral Challenge Project. Dress your loom, using your favorite method.

Weaving Notes:

The treadling is not the same as the threading. Weave hems with 10/2 cotton in the dark color, each about 1.5 inches. There are some weft stripes of a contrasting dark color on either end of the towel. Don't towels need weft stripes? The light weft is the Crab color throughout.

Finishing Method:

Wet-finish your towel and make a half-inch rolled hem.

This towel was wet-finished and dried by machine first, then hemmed. This may be stitched by hand or on the machine. I stitched the hem on the machine with a coordinating color of thread. I like to have this half inch on either end of the towel to provide an ending, a framing, or a foundation.

Finished length is 20 inches. Finished width is 14.25 inches.

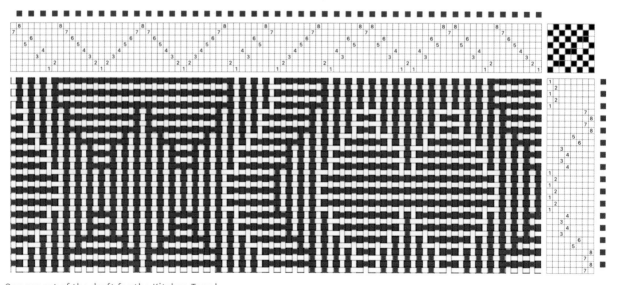

One repeat of the draft for the Kitchen Towel

CHAPTER 9 Shadow Weave Projects

Three towels

Fingertip Towel
Project Weaving Record & Notes

Draft: Marian Powell Threading Draft # 8-10-1 (1976, page 215)

Warp & Weft Yarn: 5/2 pearl cotton, 2,100 yards per pound

Warp Color: UKI Flaxon & Lunatic Fringe Yarns 5 Blue Green

Weft Color: UKI Flaxon & Lunatic Fringe Yarns 5 Blue

Sett: 15 epi

Denting: 1 per dent in a 15-dent reed

Total Ends: 193

Total Picks: I will leave the woven length to be calculated according to your own discretion, sampling, and experience.

Weaving Width in Reed: 12.87 inches

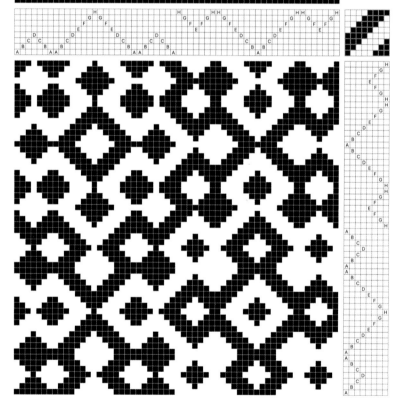

Profile draft

Fingertip Towel

Warp Winding:

I will leave the warp length to be wound to your own calculations and discretion.

Here again the threading was designed so one of the motifs was centered. This is one of my favorite motifs—sometimes called the Maltese cross. The threading represents about two and a half repeats of the Powell draft, plus eight ends added to each side to bring the dark points to the edge. This creates a diamond containing four of the crosses. See the designing notes in "Warp Winding" for the Kitchen Towel.

Follow the suggestions for winding in the Coral Challenge Project. Dress your loom, using your favorite method.

Weaving Notes:

The treadling is as drawn in. Weave hems with 10/2 cotton in a contrasting color, each about 1.5 inches. The dark warp and weft yarns for this towel are different, but very close in color. One was used in the warp and another in the weft. This adds a little spark to the cloth and may motivate a viewer to take a closer look.

Upon critiquing this textile, I have to say the motifs are a little squashed. This means I beat a little too firmly. This is a result of the narrower weaving width. There is less resistance on a narrower warp. The weft will pack in more when using the same beat you might use on a wider warp. And ultimately, I have to say this towel will dry my hands just as well, and it is still very beautiful.

Finishing Method:

Wet-finish your towel and make a half-inch rolled hem.

This towel was wet-finished and dried by machine first, then hemmed.

Finished length is 17.5 inches. Finished width is 10.75 inches.

One repeat of the draft for the Fingertip Towel

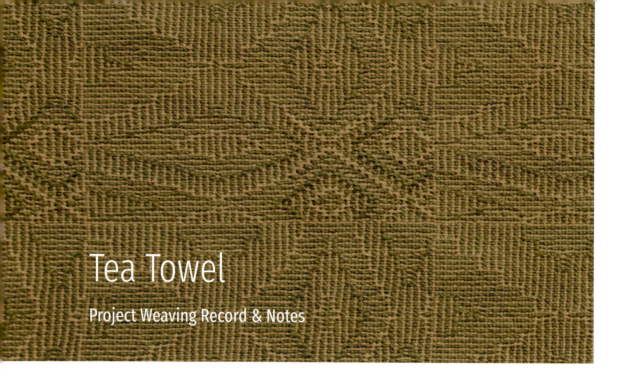

Tea Towel

Project Weaving Record & Notes

Draft: Original Draft, Profile 5

Warp Yarn: 10/2 pearl cotton, 4,200 yards per pound, from Lily Yarns

Warp Color: Avocado and Pink

Weft Yarn & Color: Same as the warp

Sett: 24 epi

Denting: 2 per dent in a 12-dent reed

Total Ends: 389

Total Picks: Adjust this length according to your own sampling and experience.

Weaving Width in Reed: 16.2 inches

Profile draft 5

Tea Towel

Warp Winding:

I will leave the warp length to be wound to your own calculations and discretion.

The yarns for this towel are from my yarn stash and are antique Lily yarns purchased at some weaver's estate sale. They are comparable to UKI colors called Peach and Peacock Green. Yes, the light is a pale pink. However, in the cloth the colors blend and the pink appears more of a natural cotton color. Isn't it fun to play with color?

The threading for the towel is four repeats of the draft.

I love this draft for exploring because it pushes designing in shadow weave in several ways. There are double light ends the center of the draft. It creates an asymmetrical motif. Weaving additional repeats of the draft creates a square motif using portions of consecutive repeats. This is a little disconcerting to wrap your mind around—there is a square, but the square is not the repeat. I could have changed the profile and the draft so the lights would be placed at the edges of the repeats, which would have created the same cloth. However, this profile was my original design, and I decided to challenge you just a bit.

Weaving Notes:

The treadling is as drawn in. There are four repeats of the draft in the treadling, plus a little more to end the towel with the point twill fashion, which is the first portion of the treadling. And in reality I am obtaining more of a rectangle than a square. This again speaks to beat. I wove this on a lighter-weight loom, so my beat was lighter. The cloth still has a wonderful hand, and I like the motifs as they are woven.

The Enigma of Shadow Weave Illuminated

Finishing Method:

Wet-finish your towel and make a half-inch rolled hem.

This towel was wet-finished and dried by machine first, then hemmed.

Finished length is 21.5 inches. Finished width is 14.5 inches.

One repeat of the draft for the Tea Towel

Once More about Finishing Shadow Weave

I'm going to repeat myself on this point because it is so important. After your weaving is done, please wet-finish your shadow weave cloth. Immersion in water will allow the characteristic texture found in the weave to adequately bloom. The details of how to wet-finish will vary depending on the fiber, the end use, and the personal preferences of the weaver. Employ your own finishing techniques and, at the very least, immerse your cloth in water to allow the shadows and light to bloom.

I hope you enjoy these projects, and I hope you have gained a few gems from the descriptions of how I work with weaving. As a teacher with a passion for sharing shadow weave, I will give you one final piece of project advice:

Pay attention to the colorway!

CHAPTER 10

A Shadow Weave Synopsis

During the research process for the writing of this book, multiple weave structures, weave techniques, or weaving concepts related to shadow weave emerged. These include color-and-weave, log cabin, parallel threadings, twill, profile or short drafts, rep weave, echo weave, block theory, units, summer & winter, overshot, crackle, extended twill, lace, and parallel shadow weave. Then the inklings related to doubleweave emerged too. This is a daunting list of related weaving concepts, but a basic understanding of all of them is necessary for successful illumination of shadow weave.

Shadow weave bags
Left: 8/4 cotton shopping bag in turquoise and charcoal, courtesy of Mary Berent. Other projects by the author.

The Lists

Personally, I relate to how Harriet Tidball created conceptual lists. Of note is her Shuttle Craft Monograph 33, called *The Handloom Weaves*, which offers a listing of weave structures. She also lists the characteristics or rules of weave structures in various publications. These lists outline what it would take to create any given weave structure.

I have followed her lead and created detailed lists for shadow weave. They are the "Shadow Weave Characteristics List" in chapter 2, "The Rules for Shadow Weave within Block Theory" in chapter 6, and "The Trouble with Shadow Weave as a Block Weave" in chapter 6.

At the beginning of my journey with shadow weave, a wise mentor asked me, "What is it that makes it shadow weave? What is the definition of shadow weave?" These questions have led me through the steps of my learning, and I encourage you to refer back to the lists I created along my path. The lists are the answers to these questions, and they give you the conceptual framework from which to approach your work with shadow weave. They will assist you to create beautiful and valid cloth.

Atwater or Powell?

A summarizing statement emerged from the many references reviewed in my research: using the Atwater method is the best method for creating and understanding shadow weave drafts from twills, and the Powell method is easiest to thread and to treadle. This summation was found so many times during the literature review that it is unclear which reference to cite. Further, Atwater shadow weave is drafted on opposites, while Powell shadow weave is drafted using the sequence of the twill line. Atwater derived her drafts from twills, and Powell used units and profiles to develop her drafts.

There is another theory existing in the weaving community. Some weavers are structure people by personal style, and some are color people. This is an oversimplification, of course, because weavers are much more complex in their approach to weaving. However, if we buy into the theory for just a moment, a general conclusion can be made related to shadow weave. Structure people are more drawn to the Atwater method of shadow weave, and color people are drawn more to the Powell method. At the very least we can say that various weavers will approach shadow weave via differing routes.

The Structure of Shadow Weave

Another question: Could shadow weave be considered a separate and distinct weave structure? Shadow weave is derived from twills in either the Atwater method or the Powell method. If it is derived from twills, it is a "twill derivative." Are twill derivatives separate and distinct structures? This question may or may not be pertinent to our weaving practice, because whatever it is, we make beautiful color-and-weave cloth with shadow weave drafts, which is the point and purpose of our weaving. Perhaps this is a philosophical concept to ponder during your meditative moments of throwing the shuttle.

Conclusion

I will continue to wonder and search for the illumination of the ultimate enigma: How did Atwater derive shadow weave? What was her path of thought and development?

Meanwhile, I have found that the enigma of shadow weave can be illuminated the more one sits at the loom with shuttle in hand, weaving the cloth. I feel Atwater, Tidball, and Powell at my elbow, smiling gently and knowingly to themselves. Or on the other hand, from what I have learned about all three of them, they are telling me exactly what they think, in no uncertain terms.

And so the theme running through my head, as I continue to learn and weave the structure of shadow weave, goes something like this:

> "It's twill. No, it's plain weave.
> It's opposite on the back.
> It has something to do with block weaves.
> It can have horizontal ribs or diagonal featherstitching.
> It can be symmetrical or asymmetrical.
> It's doubleweave.
> It's a mystery.
> It is shadow and light.
> It is an enigma for us to illuminate."

Pictured: Jenni Jimmerson

Bibliography

Atwater, Mary M. *The Shuttle-Craft Book of American Hand-weaving.* Rev. ed. New York: Macmillan, 1951. The *Shuttle-Craft Guild Bulletin* had several name changes over the years. For the discussion in this book it is considered the same publication.

Atwater, Mary M. *Shuttle-Craft Guild Bulletin* [17, no. 7] (July 1940). Basin, MT: Mary M. Atwater.

Atwater, Mary M. *Shuttle-Craft Guild Bulletin* [19, no. 2] (February 1942). Basin, MT: Mary M. Atwater.

Atwater, Mary M. *Shuttle-Craft Guild Bulletin* [19, no. 4] (April 1942). Basin, MT: Mary M. Atwater.

Atwater, Mary M. *Shuttle-Craft Guild Bulletin* [19, no. 8] (August 1942). Basin, MT: Mary M. Atwater, .

Atwater, Mary M. *Shuttle-Craft Guild Bulletin* [20, no. 5] (May 1943). Basin, MT: Mary M. Atwater.

Atwater, Mary M. *Shuttle-Craft Guild Bulletin* [20, no. 6] (June 1943). Basin, MT: Mary M. Atwater.

Atwater, Mary M. *Shuttle-Craft Guild Bulletin* [21, no. 6] (June 1944). Basin, MT: Mary M. Atwater.

Atwater, Mary M. "Upholstery Fabrics, Reps." *Shuttle-Craft Guild Bulletin* 24, no. 3 (March 1947). Basin, MT: Mary M. Atwater.

Barrett, Clotilde. *Shadow Weave and Corkscrew Weave.* Boulder, CO: Colorado Fiber Center, 1980.

Black, Mary. "Exploring the Shadow Weave." *Shuttle Craft* 36, nos. 8–9 (August/September 1959): 11–17. Kentville, NS, Canada: Kentville.

Black, Mary. "Exploring the Shadow Weave, Part II." *Shuttle Craft* 36, no. 10 (October 1959): 17–27. Kentville, NS, Canada: Kentville.

Black, Mary. *The Key to Weaving.* New York: Macmillan, 1980.

Bruland, Kris. Weaving Drafts #63823, #63827, and #62154 (2004–2018). Accessed at https://www.handweaving.net.

Cox, Vila. Warped & Wonderful. http://www.warpedandwonderful.com.

Donat, Franz. *Die farbige Gewebemusterung* ("The colored fabric pattern"). Vienna and Liepzig: A. Hartlebens Verlag, 1907. Also available online, http://www2.cs.arizona.edu/patterns/weaving/books.html#D.

Hartshorn, Linda. "Shedding Light on Shadow Weave." *Heddlecraft* 1, no. 3 (May/June 2016). Tokeland, WA: Spady Studio

Keasbey, Doramay. *Pattern Techniques for Handweavers.* Eugene, OR: Doramay Keasbey, 2005.

Lambert, Patricia, Barbara Staepelaere, and Mary G. Fry. *Color and Fiber.* West Chester, PA: Schiffer, 1986.

Landis, Lucille. *Twills and Twill Derivatives.* Greenwich, CT: Lucille Landis, 1977.

Lang, Elizabeth, and Erica Dakin Voolich. *Parallel Shadow Weave.* Boston: Weavers' Guild of Boston, 1987.

Lauer, David A. *Design Basics.* 2nd ed. New York: Holt, Reinhold and Watson, 1985. First published in 1979.

Lunatic Fringe Yarns. https://lunaticfringeyarns.com.

Mary Meigs Atwater Weaver's Guild of Utah. http://www.mmawg.org/Bulletin.htm.

O'Connor, Paul R. *Loom-Controlled Double Weave: From the Notebook of a Double Weaver.* Saint Paul, MN: Dos Tejedoras Fiber Arts, 1992.

Powell, Marian. *1000 (+) Patterns in 4, 6, and 8 Harness Shadow Weaves.* 2nd ed. McMinnville, OR: Robin and Russ Handweavers, 1980. First published in 1976.

Powell, Marian. *Multi Harness and Four Harness Shadow Weave Pamphlets.* Perry, IA: Marian Powell, n.d., ca. 1965. One pamphlet threading in the sample collection of Mary Berent, master weaver. Twenty-seven pamphlet threadings in the sample collection of Rebecca Winter, master weaver.

Powell, Marian. "Shadow Weave Offers an Opportunity for Many Variations." *Handweaver & Craftsman* 12, no. 3 (Summer 1961): 20–22. Kutztown, PA: Handweaver & Craftsman.

Powell, Marian. "Shadow Weave Conversion." *Shuttle Craft* 37, no. 3 (March 1960): 4–9. Kentville, NS, Canada: Kentville.

Powell, Marian. "Shadow Weave Conversion, Part II." *Shuttle Craft* 37, no. 4 (April 1960): 11–17. Kentville, NS, Canada: Kentville.

Powell, Marian. "Shadow Weave Conversion, Part III." *Shuttle Craft* 37, no. 5 (May 1960): 18–22. Kentville, NS, Canada: Kentville.

Strickler, Carol, ed. *A Weaver's Book of 8-Shaft Patterns.* Loveland, CO: Interweave, 1991.

Tidball, Harriet. Additions by Virginia I. Harvey. *The Handloom Weaves.* Enlarged 2nd ed. Shuttle Craft Guild Monograph 33. Coupeville, WA: Shuttle Craft Books, 1984. First published in 1957.

Tidball, Harriet. "The Shadow Weave." *Shuttle Craft Guild Handweaver's Bulletin* 30, no. 7 (July 1953): 1–9. Virginia City, MT: Harriet and Martin Tidball, Shuttle Craft Guild.

van der Hoogt, Madelyn. *The Complete Book of Drafting for Handweavers.* Coupeville, WA: Shuttle Craft Books, 1993.

Watson, William. *Textile Design and Colour.* London: Longmans, Green, 1912.

WEBS, America's Yarn Store. https://www.yarn.com.

Windeknecht, Margaret B., and Thomas Windeknecht. *Color-and-Weave.* New York: Van Nostrand Reinhold, 1981.

Appendix A

Shadow Weave Sett Chart

Weavers have access to many sett charts. You will find that the information offered in this one will be similar to others you find. These setts have been tested and sampled specifically for shadow weave. Space has been included at the end of the chart for you to add your own favorite yarns.

Yarn	Sett (ends per inch)
20/2 cotton	36
10/2 cotton	24
5/2 cotton	15
5/2 cotton for rep weave	40
3/2 cotton	12
8/2 cotton	20
8/4 cotton	12 to 15
Worsted weight cotton	8 to 12
8/2 Tencel	20 to 24
16/2 linen	18
2/30 silk	30
Harrisville Shetland 2-ply wool	12 to 15
2/20 JaggerSpun Maine Line wool	24

Appendix B

Additional Atwater Drafts

In the April 1942 *Shuttle-Craft Guild Bulletin*, there are three shadow weave drafts. Atwater offered these drafts after requests came from guild members for more shadow weave. Drafts (a) through (d) are drafts for other weaves appropriate for drapery fabrics, which was the main topic of that issue.

For the shadow weave drafts, no separate treadling was offered, so they are shown here as drawn in.

Draft indicated in April 1942 as (e)

Appendix B

Atwater calls draft (e) "a 'Dornik-Herringbone' arrangement of this weave" (April 1942, page 4).

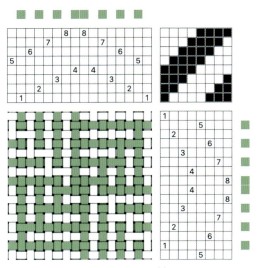

Draft indicated in April 1942 as (f)

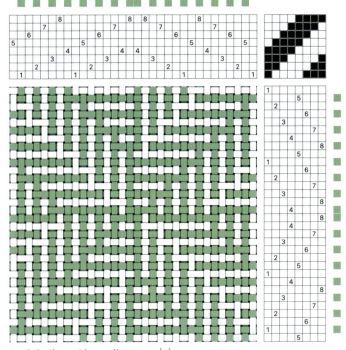

Draft indicated in April 1942 as (g)

171

Appendix B

In all three of these drafts, both darks and lights are doubled. The points are asymmetrical.

The next publication in the *Shuttle-Craft Guild Bulletin* about shadow weave was in May 1943. A year later, it is apparent that Atwater had done a bit of work on shadow weave, and there is a different type of management of the points in the drafts. We see the points here as having a single thread at the points, making them symmetrical. Treadlings are written in text format, and interestingly, none of these drafts are presented as drawn in.

Draft indicated in May 1943 as No. 1

Appendix B

The threading points pivot on 1 and 8. The treadling points pivot on 5. This draft is very similar to the drafts in the February 1942 article.

Draft indicated in May 1943 as No. 2

Appendix B

Here we find a different management of the points. Again, they are symmetrical.

This draft is a combination of switch draft and regular shadow weave.

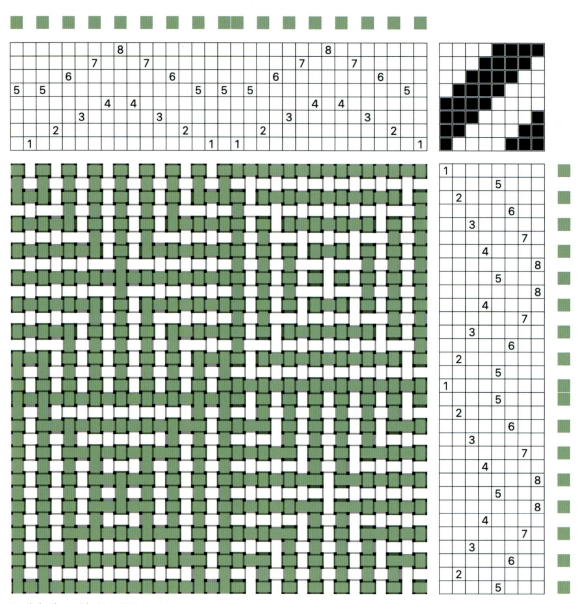

Draft indicated in May 1943 as No. 3

Appendix B

This is an asymmetrical draft.

Draft indicated in May 1943 as No. 4

Appendix B

Draft indicated in May 1943 as No. 5

Again, we see a combination draft.

Atwater also offered a description of creating borders on these drafts. Below is an example of draft no. 5 with this feature. She described working with the new 4/4 cotton Lily yarn and found it to be "clumsy" for most of their usual weaves. She said it worked well with shadow weave and could be used for making blankets or throws, and borders enhance weaving projects such as these.

Draft indicated in May 1943 as No. 5, with a border

Appendix B

The issue of the *Shuttle-Craft Guild Bulletin* published the next month, June 1943, included two additional drafts on four shafts. There was not room for these drafts in the May issue, according to Atwater.

Draft indicated in June 1943 as (d)

The draft (e) draft contains two repeats of the pattern, and this was how Atwater published it.

Draft indicated in June 1943 as (e)

Appendix B

Three more threadings of "the shadow weave" were offered by Atwater in the June 1944 issue of the *Shuttle-Craft Guild Bulletin*. This issue focused on offering drafts suitable for "dress-fabric," suitings, or other clothing fabrics. Drafts (a) and (e) were in weaves other than shadow weave. Drafts (b), (c), and (d) were designated as "shadow weave" on the draft page. She also gave three treadling options for (b), and two treadling options for (c). She recommended using finer cotton yarns for the purposes outlined, such as 20/2 or 24/3 cotton.

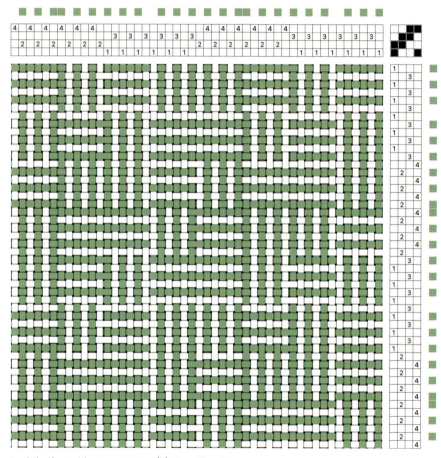

Draft indicated in June 1944 as (b), treadling #1

Appendix B

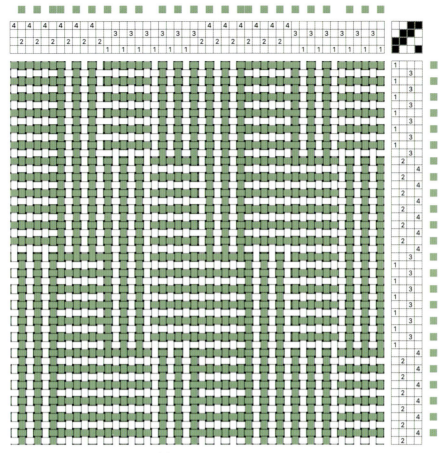

Draft indicated in June 1944 as (b), treadling #2

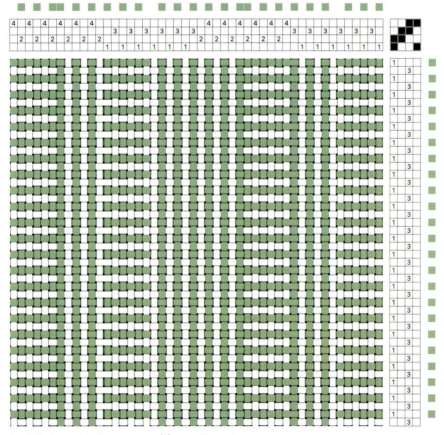

Draft indicated in June 1944 as (b), treadling #3

Appendix B

Draft indicated in June 1944 as (c), treadling #1

Appendix B

The draft (c), treadling #2, has a more overall patterning, which is more appropriate for suitings, especially in finer threads.

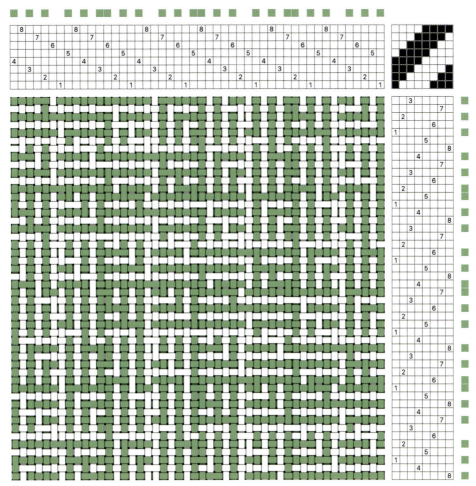

Draft indicated in June 1944 as (c), treadling #2

183

Appendix B

The treadling in (d) is the same as (c), #1, from the same issue. This weave makes an interesting undulating diagonal-stripe motif.

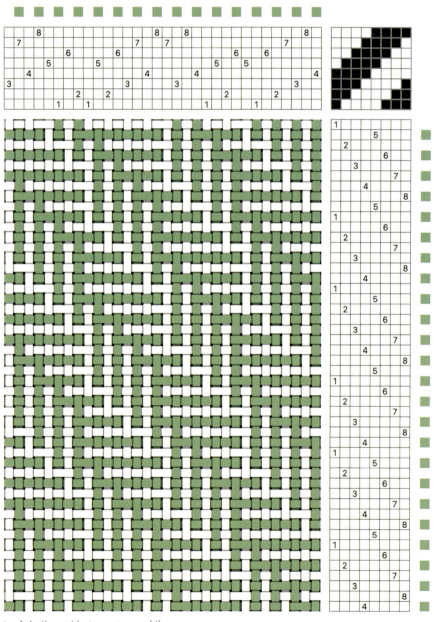

Draft indicated in June 1944 as (d)

Appendix B

Mary Black published an article about shadow weave in *Shuttle Craft*, October 1959. She said she was in possession of some of Atwater's samples at the time, and the draft shown next is developed from Black's description. She said the sample colors were black and tan for the warp, white and magenta for the weft.

This draft represents two repeats of both the threading and the treadling.

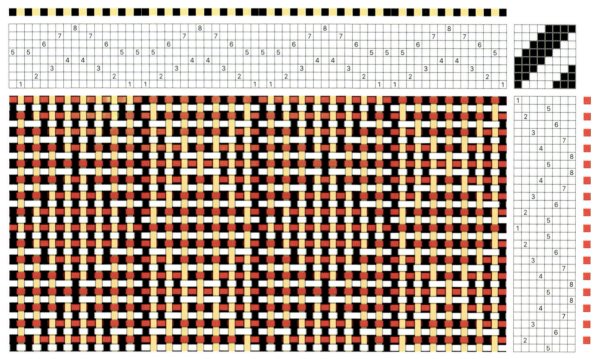

Draft indicated in October 1959 as #8, using the colors described by Atwater

Appendix B

The final issue of the *Shuttle Craft* containing shadow weave drafts was in June/July 1960. This article was again by Black and continued her "Exploring of shadow weave." She reported there had been a lot of interest and correspondence about shadow weave as a result of her previous articles in *Shuttle Craft*. One guild member, Mrs. Winifred Jones, loaned a shadow weave book of drafts and samples to Black for review. One of the samples was woven from a draft given directly to Mrs. Jones by Atwater. This draft had not been previously published.

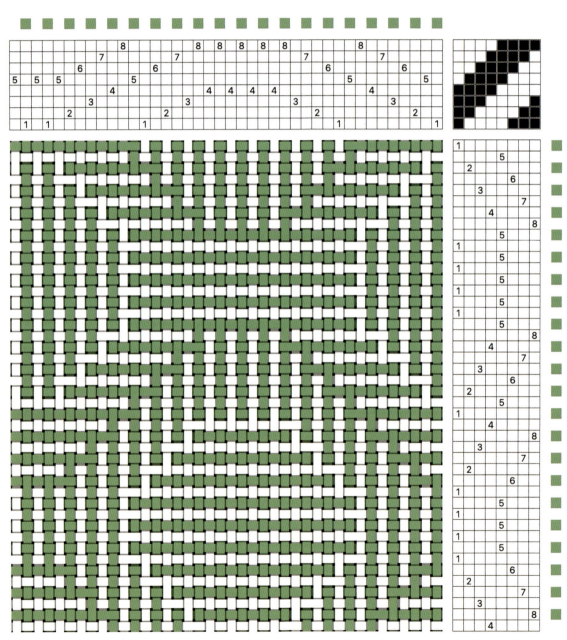

Draft published in June/July 1960

Here again this draft is not as drawn in, and it creates an all-over patterning of circles.

Three repeats of the draft published in June/July 1960

Appendix C

Three Methods of Creating the Same Exact Cloth

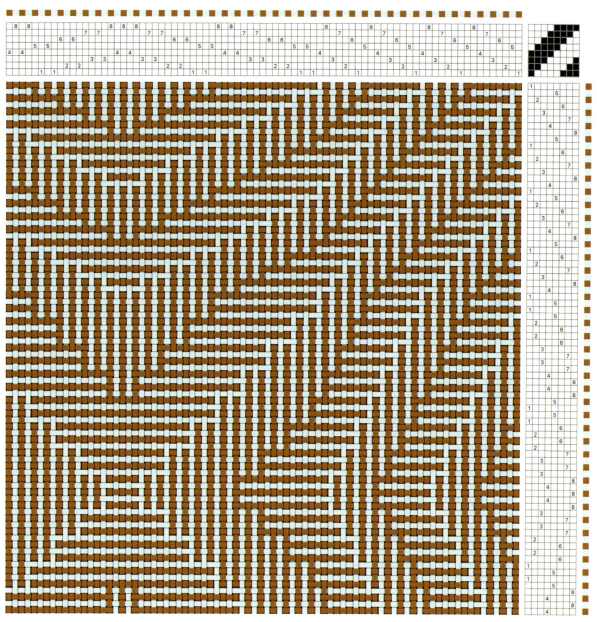

Atwater shadow weave method

Appendix C

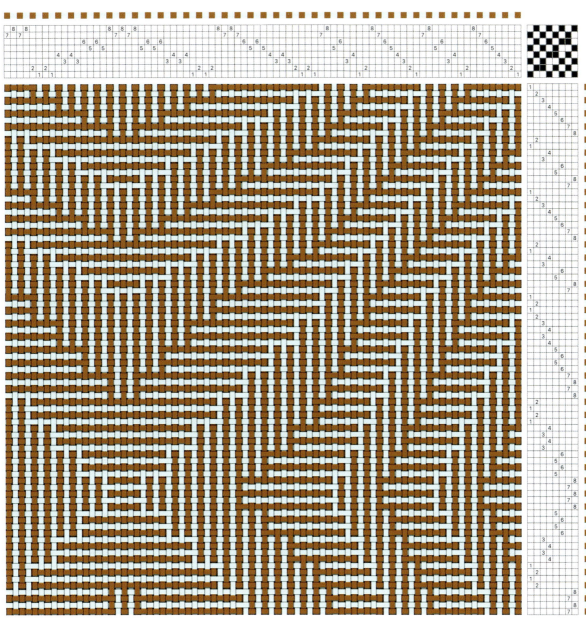

Powell shadow weave method

Appendix C

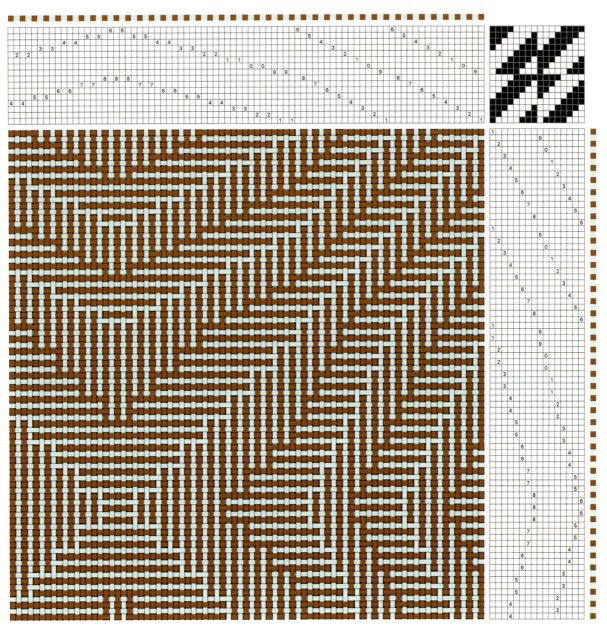

Parallel shadow weave method

Index

as drawn in, 48, 61, 100, 105, 108, 142, 152, 156
Atwater drafts. *See* drafts
Atwater, Mary Meigs, 18, 23

Barrett, Clotilde, 18, 23
Black, Mary, 18, 23, 129, 185
block weave
    Atwater units, 84
    background block, 81, 82, 91, 96, 97
    pattern block, 81, 82, 91, 96, 97
    Powell units, 85
    rules, 96
    shared units, 87–89
    units weave together, 91–93

Chown, Joyce, 23
color-and-weave, 17, 32, 36, 37, 39, 55, 85, 95, 96, 102, 104, 123
    definition, 35
contrast
    color intensity, 116
    hue, 36, 37, 107, 116
    scale, 116, 121
    simultaneous, 38
    texture, 116, 123
    value, 32, 35, 36, 38, 39, 53, 116, 119, 123

design element
    contrast (*see* contrast)
    distance, 39
    hue (*see* hue)
    optical mixing, 38
    scale, 38, 113
    value (*see* value)
Donat, Franz, 19
doubleweave, 33, 66–71, 125–129
drafts
    4-shaft, 54, 64, 69, 78, 93, 126, 176, 177, 178, 179, 180, 181, 182, 183
    6-shaft, 19, 29, 39, 42, 47, 79, 86, 87, 88, 89, 93, 94, 100, 101, 102, 103, 104, 107, 108, 113, 116, 138
    8-shaft, 31, 54–57, 61, 63, 66, 67, 74, 77, 90–92, 105, 106, 109–112, 119, 120, 143, 146, 150, 154, 158, 170–175, 184–189
    12-shaft, 114
    16-shaft, 190
    asymmetrical, 33, 83, 89–90, 97, 175
    Atwater, 52–58, 61–67, 69, 70, 74, 78, 79, 89, 170–187, 188
    conventions, 39–40
    conversion to Powell, 73–79
    interlocking, 23
    Powell, 19, 29, 31, 39, 41, 42, 47, 77, 78, 79, 86, 87, 88, 89, 90, 92, 93, 94, 100, 010, 102, 103, 104, 106, 107, 108, 109, 111, 112, 113, 114, 116, 119, 120, 126, 136, 138, 149, 150, 152,154
    profile, 93, 105, 110, 136, 140, 144, 149, 152, 156
    reversal adjustments, 87–89, 96, 97, 110
    structure, 40, 47, 55, 58, 62, 65, 66, 70, 75, 95
    switch, 102–104
    symmetrical, 86–89, 96, 97, 100, 110
    unidirectional, 19, 29, 53, 55, 74, 77–79, 86

enigma, 12–13, 18, 97, 95, 128, 129, 164
extended shadow weave, 100–101

featherstitching, 28–33, 42, 86, 89–90, 100, 102–104, 107, 110, 113, 127–128
finishing fabric, 133, 139, 159

Handweaver & Craftsman, 24
Hartshorn, Linda, 18, 23
hatching, 18, 25, 28, 32, 33, 42, 82, 91–93, 95, 96, 97, 102, 107, 110, 113
hue, 36–38, 116

Keasbey, Doramay, 18, 23, 126

lace, 114

multiple shaft shadow weave, 20, 24, 48, 113

op art, 38

parallel shadow weave, 23, 48, 113, 190
plain weave, 23, 28, 31, 32, 33, 38, 41, 43, 46, 48, 69, 81, 113, 127, 128
Powell draft conversion, 73–79
Powell drafts. *See* drafts
Powell, Marian, 18, 24–25, 81, 102, 105, 123

Index

rep weave, 17, 18, 22, 98, 123, 126, 128–129, 168

scarf, 136, 140, 144
selvages
    alternate management method, 43–46
    floating, 43
sett, 32, 121, 132, 139, 168
shadow and light, 114, 164
shadow weave
    characteristics, 23, 27, 28–29, 32–33, 162
    rules, 32–33, 96–97, 113
    units (see units)
Shuttle-Craft Guild Bulletin, 18, 23, 28, 31, 55–71, 126, 128–129, 170–186
summer & winter, 81, 83

Tidball, Harriet, 18, 23, 28, 29, 31, 33, 40, 88, 123, 127, 128, 162
tie-up
    Atwater, 32, 54, 55, 74
    fancy twill, 19, 20, 22
    Powell, 79
    rising shed, 41
    sinking shed, 41, 42
towel, 148, 152, 156

twill
    broken twill fashion, 50, 55, 107
    circles, 52, 53, 86
    extended, 48–49, 64
    point, 33, 48–49, 87
    point twill fashion, 46–47, 86, 87–89, 96–97, 100–101
    straight, 28, 48
    straight twill fashion, 29, 52–53, 55, 73–79, 83, 85, 100, 126, 127

unit weave, 17, 33, 81, 83, 86, 89, 91, 97
unit(s), 53, 83, 86–97, 100, 105–110, 162

valid cloth, 41, 59, 68, 97, 108, 128, 162
value, 36, 37, 38, 53, 89, 95, 104, 107, 121
van der Hoogt, Madelyn, 18, 23, 126

Watson, William, 20–22
weave
    3-color, 116–117
    4-color, 117–120
    balanced, 32, 55, 91, 92, 96, 121–123
    warp-faced, 122, 129
Windeknecht, Margaret & Thomas, 33

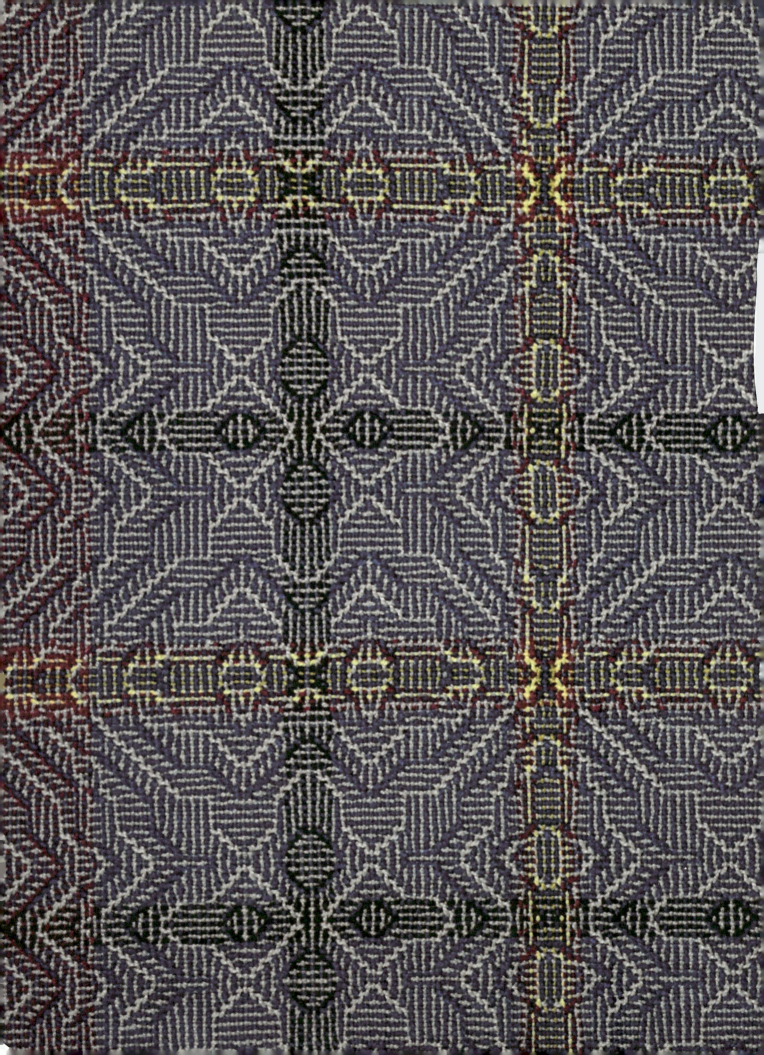